The Lord's Freedman

The Dynamic Message of Paul

The Lord's Freedman

The Dynamic Message of Paul

Keith W. Lamb

Treasure House

An Imprint of

Destiny Image Publishers, Inc. ®
P.O. Box 310
Shippensburg, PA 17257-0310

ISBN 1-56043-829-0

For Worldwide Distribution
Printed in the U.S.A.

Treasure House books are available through these fine distributors outside the United States:

Christian Growth, Inc.,
Jalan Kilang-Timor, Singapore 0315

Lifestream
Nottingham, England

Rhema Ministries Trading
Randburg, South Africa

Salvation Book Centre
Petaling, Jaya, Malaysia

Successful Christian Living
Capetown, Rep. of South Africa

Vine Christian Centre
Mid Glamorgan, Wales, United Kingdom

Vision Resources
Ponsonby, Auckland, New Zealand

WA Buchanan Company
Geebung, Queensland, Australia

Word Alive
Niverville, Manitoba, Canada

Inside the U.S., call toll free to order:
1-800-722-6774

Acknowledgment

With sincerest gratitude, I wish to thank Jean Hartzell, Mary Ann Rowan, and Patricia Arnold, who gave of their talents and labor in transcribing and editing these pages. I also thank Linda Fleetwood for her idea for the cover.

Contents

Introduction

*For he that is called in the Lord, being a serv-
ant, is the Lord's freeman: likewise also he that
is called, being free, is Christ's servant
(1 Corinthians 7:22).*

When Paul penned these words to the church at
Corinth, he was outlining the core of his message to
the Body of Christ. He wanted the people of God to
know that liberty comes through and is made secure
in the Lordship of Jesus Christ. The expression "the
Lord's freeman [or more properly, *freedman*]" would
suggest that true freedom is only to be realized when
one lives out his or her life under the authority of
Jesus Christ. Moreover, to be the servant of the Christ
(more accurately, the *Anointed*) is to be energized to
walk in the same anointing that was on Him.

To be a freed man is to be loosed from the bondage
of the past to a new liberty in the present and in the
future. The believer in Christ is freed from the bondage of sin, but often enters another bondage to the

law and the "letter." The law is that righteous standard which God requires, but which is not attainable through human effort. The letter is the words of God found in both the Old and New Testament (or Covenant), which are turned into more "rules to live by." In Second Corinthians 3:6 Paul said, "...the new testament; [which is] not of the letter, but of the spirit: for the letter killeth, but the spirit giveth life." God, through Christ, has sent the Holy Spirit into our hearts so the righteous standard of the law could be fulfilled in us.

If we, as believers, can see that God's standard has been achieved, we enter the liberty and joy that rightfully belongs to a slave who has been set free. Paul said in Romans 6 that we, as believers in Christ Jesus, were slaves to sin. In Galatians 5:1 he warns us not to be entangled again in the bondage of law. The Spirit brings abundant life, but the efforts of the flesh to live by the law profits nothing.

I pray that the words of this book, inadequate as they may be, will help you more fully understand and enjoy the freedom our Father has set before us.

Chapter 1

The Lord's Freedman

Paul, Apostle to the Gentiles

Paul, as the apostle to the Gentiles, carried out a special and unique mission for God, a mission of great importance. We are privileged to view this unique ministry through the letters, or epistles, that Paul wrote to the churches he founded. We will take up our vantage point for his ministry in the letter he wrote to the church at Galatia. What we learn and the information we examine in it will be supported from other letters he wrote during the term of his life and ministry.

First of all, in Second Timothy 3:16 the apostle acknowledges the efficacy of Scripture when he says "All scripture is given by inspiration of God, and is profitable for doctrine, for reproof, for correction, for instruction in righteousness." As we read Paul's epistles, we find that they can be divided into four categories: doctrine, reproof, correction, and instruction.

1

Often the presentations overlap from one area to another. For example, Romans addresses doctrine; First and Second Corinthians offer reproof; Galatians through Second Thessalonians make corrections; and First Timothy through Philemon provide instructions in righteousness.

The focus of this book, the Epistle to the Galatians, falls into the category of correction. The Galatians started well, but they ran into obstacles that threatened their continued growth. Paul said, "Who did hinder you?" (Gal. 5:7) By what had they been hindered? What was changing in their walk as a result of that hindrance? What was Paul trying to correct? How serious was it? Those are the concerns of this epistle.

Galatians is the Gentile counterpart of the Epistle to the Hebrews. The same problems we find in Hebrews, Paul addresses in his letter to the Galatians. The root of this problem, in both cases, is primarily legalism or, more than that, religious self-effort. The Book of Hebrews points out an unwillingness to abandon those efforts that produce only dead works and to go forward to serve God in the Spirit rather than under the works of the law. That epistle was written to the Jewish believers in order to teach them to stop being Hebrews. The Epistle to the Galatians was written to the Gentile believers in order to rescue them from the trap and the death-dealing snare of self-righteous effort.

Religious self-effort was not a problem for the Galatians in the beginning. They walked in liberty and in step with the Holy Spirit. Since they were not bound by the laws of the Jews, they started out free from the demands the law imposed. These young believers walked with the Lord in a special relationship, doing the will of God from the heart.

Then from Jerusalem came Judaisers (Christians with a Jewish background). They demanded that the believers in Galatia adhere to the legalistic system of the Jews. That is why Paul said to them, "You did run well, who hindered you?" (see Gal. 5:7) Paul often used imagery that the Gentiles could understand, and I like to think Paul was saying, "You were staying in your lane." When he spoke of running well, he was alluding to the Grecian games where each runner is required to stay in his own lane. As in these same races today, if a runner gets out of his or her lane, that runner is disqualified. Paul is saying, "You ran well; who pushed you out of your lane?" He is warning them not to become disqualified from the race.

This analogy to the Greek races illustrates the believer's loss or victorious gain in the day of the Lord Jesus Christ. You may remember the story of Ben Hur. After Yahuda Ben Hur had won the chariot race, he was brought before the judgment seat to receive his crown of victory. This seat was the Bemah, a raised platform, which is similar to Paul's description of the judgment seat of Christ. The crown given at the games was a laurel wreath signifying victory. This wreath of victory, *stephanos* in the Greek, is the center of Paul's concern. Every believer will receive his of her crown at the bemah seat of Christ (see 2 Cor. 5:10). These Galatian believers had been running the race well. Now the legalists had come to them and were trying to force them out of their lane. They were in danger of losing their crown of victory, which is obtained by grace through faith (see Rom. 11:6; Eph. 2:8).

Paul's Ministry and Authority

Before we deal with the issue of law and legalism, let us first look at Paul's ministry and the authority he had received as an apostle. He begins his Epistle to the Galatians:

Paul, an apostle (not sent from men, nor through the agency of man, but through Jesus Christ, and God the Father, who raised Him from the dead), and all the brethren who are with me, to the churches of Galatia: Grace to you and peace from God our Father, and the Lord Jesus Christ, who gave Himself for our sins, that He might deliver us out of this present evil age, according to the will of our God and Father, to whom be the glory forevermore. Amen (Galatians 1:1-5 NAS).

Notice the portion of these verses that appear in parentheses. "...not sent from men, nor through the agency of man, but through Jesus Christ, and God the Father, who raised Him from the dead...." Paul is contrasting the way he was called into his

4

apostleship with the manner in which many apostles are set aside. For example, when he speaks of Epaphroditus, who came to him in Philippi, he refers to him as his messenger (apostle). (See Philippians 2:25.) Now Epaphroditus is a New Testament apostle, but he received his position because man set him into that office. Paul is alerting us to the fact that he was not set into the office of apostle by any man, but by Jesus Christ.

The evidence of Paul's commission is recorded in the ninth chapter of Acts. Paul was, at the time, named Saul and was the great persecutor of the Church. He was travelling toward Damascus to arrest the followers of "the way." Entering into the service of the Lord Jesus Christ was the furtherest thing from his mind. Little did he know that God had sovereignly chosen him before he was born for the mantle that would soon be placed upon him (see Gal. 1:15). Paul testifies to his conversion when he is called before King Agrippa:

> At midday, O King, I saw on the way a light from heaven, brighter than the sun, shining all around me and those who were journeying with me. And when we had all fallen to the ground, I heard a voice saying to me in the Hebrew dialect, "Saul, Saul, why are you persecuting Me? It is hard for you to kick against the goads." And I said, "Who art Thou, Lord?" And the Lord said, "I am Jesus whom you are persecuting. But arise, and stand on your feet; for this

purpose I have appeared to you, to appoint you a minister and a witness not only to the things which you have seen, but also to the things in which I will appear to you; delivering you from the Jewish people and from the Gentiles, to whom I am sending you, to open their eyes so that they may turn from darkness to light and from the dominion of Satan to God, in order that they may receive forgiveness of sins and an inheritance among those who have been sanctified by faith in Me" (Acts 26:13-18 NAS).

In commissioning Paul as an apostle to the Gentiles, God said, "I'm going to send you to the Gentiles to open their eyes, to turn them from darkness to light, to turn them from the power of Satan unto God, that the Gentiles might receive forgiveness of sins and an inheritance among those who are sanctified."

You may recall that Peter, not Paul, had the privilege of first bringing the gospel to the Gentiles. It was also Peter to whom Jesus committed the keys of the Kingdom. Peter alluded to this fact when he entered the house of Cornelius, preached the gospel to this Roman, and saw the Holy Spirit fall on those in the house (see Acts 10). But it was the apostle Paul who became the apostle to the Gentiles. It was Paul who was given the light to bring them from the power of satan and into liberty as children of God (see Eph. 3:1-8). God had truly given Paul a special mission, a mission that would turn him from a destiny of infamy as a persecutor of God's people, to a destiny of greatness as the apostle to the Gentiles.

Old Testament and New Testament Parallels

A number of hints of this special mission exist in the Old Testament when you compare the ministry of Paul and the ministry of Moses. Often in Scripture, we find parallels between men of the Old Testament and men of the New Testament. I have found that to be true of Moses and Paul. For example, consider the following:

- Both of these men were called by God from the womb. Both had a direct revelation from the Lord.
- Both were made stewards of this revelation and were charged with carrying out God's instructions.
- Both were rejected by their brethren.
- Both spent a period of time in the desert to pray and to learn more of God's plan.
- Both were willing to die as a substitute or vicarious offering for God's people.
- Both met the Lord through a glorious visitation.
- Both were noted for a physical impediment (speech and sight).

As you follow the details of their ministries, the parallels become even more apparent. Why is this significant? Moses ushered in the age or dispensation of the law, while Paul introduced the Gentiles to the dispensation of grace, which was freedom from the law. God did not give the law to anyone else; He gave it to Moses. God gave His revelation for the Church to Paul.

Paul the Builder

Isn't it also interesting how the Lord often assigned the mission of early disciples as a reflection of their occupation? For example, when the Lord called Peter, he was catching fish. He went on to be an evangelist, a fisher of men. When the Lord called John, he was mending nets. He stood out in his ministry as the mender of the Body of Christ. "I have no greater joy," he said, "than to hear that my children walk in truth" (3 Jn. 4). This is the binding together of the Body. "For this is the message that ye heard from the beginning, that we should love one another" (1 Jn. 3:11).

Paul was a tent maker. God committed to him the task of building the Church. "According to the grace of God which is given unto me, as a wise master-builder, I have laid the foundation, and another buildeth thereon. But let every man take heed how he buildeth thereupon" (1 Cor. 3:10). We can see each of these three apostles in the words of Jesus (Jn. 14:6): "I am the way"—is Peter; "I am the truth"—is John; "I am the life"—is Paul. Although these apostles spoke about every aspect of the gospel, each seemed to emphasize these aspects in his own particular manner, making them peculiar to their individual ministries. This is not to say that these men did not speak to other areas, just that their emphases were primarily the course of their individual ministries.

As a builder concerned with the life of the structure he was building, Paul, because his unique position relative to the revelation of the grace of God, was concerned about what he saw in the church at Galatia. The warning begins in chapter 1, verse 6. Paul is always alert for anyone who might enter in and try to pervert or counterfeit the message God had delivered to the Church through him.

Hebrews 11:10 reads, "For he [Abraham] looked for a city which hath foundations, whose builder and maker is God." The word *builder* can also be translated "designer." Often we see signs advertising homes where the contractor is the designer/builder. From the Master Designer/Builder came the ideas, fashioned in His heart, from which the Church was molded. The Designer then is the Father. Now the Maker, on the other hand, is the Holy Spirit. How do we know this? Paul tells us that we are co-laborers with God (see 1 Cor. 3:9). Since it is the person of the Holy Spirit who empowers the believer and energizes him for the work of the ministry, this "Maker" (in Greek it often means "public worker") must be the third Person of the Godhead.

In Matthew 16:18 we also find the word *build*. Jesus said, "Upon this rock I will build My church." In this case the word is appropriately translated. It is the same word used in Acts 7:47 about Solomon, who built the temple. Solomon did not go out and physically lay stones, but he was responsible for building the temple as well as the manner in which it was built. Likewise, Jesus is the Head over the Body and the Foreman of the construction of the building of God. Thus we see how the triune God is active in building this holy temple of the Lord.

As for the building, some have identified it with the Holy City, the New Jerusalem that descends from God out of Heaven like a bride. (See Revelation 21:2.) Certainly the Holy City will have the characteristics of the bride because the bride will live there. It is fashioned *as* a bride adorned for the bridegroom, Jesus.

To put this in perspective, the designer is responsible for the original plan. He gives the plan to the builder, who in turn charges the public worker with the responsibility of getting the job done. However, in order for the public worker (the Holy Spirit) to come up with a finished product, another worker is required. He is called the architect. We find a word in the New Testament, *masterbuilder*, which is translated from the Greek word *archatecton*. It is a combination of two Greek words, *arxa* and *tekton*, and means "chief carpenter." In effect, God is saying that He will provide a chief carpenter to take from the Holy Spirit what was thought of in the heart of the Father, and write it down on paper so we will have a blueprint to follow. Then we, the members of His Body, can start building as we labor together with God.

The architect of the law was Moses. God took him up into the mount and said, "Now, Moses, this is what I want you to tell them." He wrote that down. Then God said, "This is what it looks like," and God showed it to him. Moses then returned to the people as a true architect and said, "I have the print. I saw what it looks like and I know how we are supposed to build it." God even said, "See—that thou make all things according to the pattern shewed to thee in the mount" (Heb. 8:5b).

Paul, like Moses, received his instructions from God. He was taken by the Lord into the third heaven and shown things not lawful to be uttered (see 2 Cor. 12:2-4). Among these things was the plan for the Church, which is His Body. Thus Paul could say, "I, as a wise masterbuilder and chief carpenter, who received the print from the Builder, Jesus Christ, will now give you the design for the building of God, the habitation of God by the Spirit." We are now building that holy structure in accordance with the plans given to Paul and set forth by him in his 14 epistles. (I include the Epistle to the Hebrews in this count). Although the Holy Spirit has given us much truth through the other New Testament writers, only through Paul do we receive the structure of the Church.

Paul's Message

It is necessary, even imperative, for the gospel to be preached where the gospel is needed. By *the gospel*, I mean the gospel of the redeeming grace of God.

But if we would go on to perfection, we must proceed to the gospel of salvation that Paul refers to in his Epistle to the Romans. Then we can discover what is in store for the believer after redemption. You see, after the foundation is laid, we must get on with the rest of the construction.

I like to look at it this way. Suppose a man buys something from a department store, but it is not assembled. He sits down and reads the directions, looks at all the diagrams, goes over the directions again, and commits everything to memory. He wants to be sure the product he has bought is assembled correctly so it will function and accomplish the job he bought it to do.

Today many believers do much the same thing—they memorize the directions for building the Church. Unfortunately, we stopped at this point. Unlike the man who went on to assemble and use his product, we simply memorized the directions. We judge maturity in the Lord by how well each of us knows the Scriptures. However, simply knowing the Scriptures does not determine maturity in the Lord. Maturity is determined by how well the truth works in one's life. If I know how to put the apparatus together, but don't assemble it, what value is it? I say, "No value at all." I should not have wasted all that time reading and memorizing if I was not going to assemble the product.

What God does through the process of salvation is work on me to put the building together. I believe this is the central issue in Paul's gospel. "For it is God which worketh in you both to will and to do of His good pleasure" (Phil. 2:13). In Second Timothy 3:17 he says, "That the man of God may be perfect [some stop here], throughly furnished [others stop here] unto all good works [few have gotten this far]." The process is not working for many because they are not following Paul's instructions. In order to build the building, one must use the proper tools. Those tools were given to us by Paul.

Can you imagine Solomon trying to build the temple without the proper equipment? By the same token, neither can the building of God's Church be finished without proper directions and the tools prescribed by the epistles of Paul. The architect has spoken the words of the "Builder and Maker." Now we must take care to hear and follow his plan.

Paul, Unique Among the Apostles

I believe Paul is a unique apostle. There are many apostles who were not one of the original 12. In fact, 22 apostles are named in the New Testament. When the phrase "the 12" is used, however, it always refers to the original 12 apostles. Those 12 occupy a special place in the history of the Church and in the life of Jesus Christ. Other New Testament men mentioned as apostles include Timothy, Silas, Barnabas, and Epaphroditus.

Some pastors and teachers suggest that when the first apostles chose Matthias in Acts 1, the choice was wrong or it was not God's choice. They argue that the Holy Spirit had not yet come and therefore the apostles "preempted the Lord" by not waiting on Him. These pastors and teachers go on to suggest that God intended Paul to fill the place left vacant by Judas. Nowhere does the Word of God suggest such a concept. Quite the contrary!

Luke wrote the Book of Acts well after the events of Pentecost. Luke did not become a disciple until the events described in Acts 16. Was Luke familiar with the early history of the Church, the movement of the disciples, and the work of Jesus? When addressing his friend Theophilus in the Gospel of Luke, he suggests that he had knowledge of those early events (see Lk. 1:3). The expression, "from the very first," explains this point. The Greek word *anoothen* can be translated as "from above." Luke is telling us that he received this message by Divine inspiration. He did not receive it through consultation with the other disciples. If this is true of his Gospel account, then his account in the Book of Acts, also addressed to Theophilus, would carry the same authority. The Book of Acts, like the Gospel of Luke, was written under the inspiration of the Holy Spirit. We can receive both messages as correct and be confident of Luke's accounts.

In Acts 2:14, when Peter begins to speak, Matthias had already been chosen to fill Judas' spot. The verse reads, "But Peter, standing up with the eleven, lifted up his voice, and said...." Therefore, Peter must have numbered Matthias as one of the original

12, since he stood with 11. Keep in mind that no objection was offered at the time Matthias was chosen. So, on the Day of Pentecost, Luke includes him with the other apostles. I must conclude that he was numbered with the 12 by Peter with God's approval.

If you are prone to question the casting of lots as a means of selection, let me point out that the practice was used in the Old Testament as a way of finding the mind of God. An example of this practice can be found in the story of Jonah. Jonah was hiding from God on a ship. The ship's crew was made up of unbelieving Gentiles, each one calling on his god. The sailors cast lots to see who was the cause of the storm, and God honored the lot. In effect He said, "There he is, My man, down in the hold of the ship." Thus this same practice would not be an unusual choice for the disciples. The Holy Spirit, speaking through Luke, confirms the selection, saying, "...and [Matthias] was numbered with the eleven apostles" (Acts 1:26b).

Paul and Peter

Jesus' testimony to those who were with Him states that 12 of them would sit on 12 thrones judging the 12 tribes of Israel (see Mt. 19:28). This statement was never made to the apostle Paul. His position in the family of God is relative to the Body of Christ, which is made up largely of Gentiles. The Book of Acts testifies to that quite beautifully. After the ninth chapter of Acts, the other disciples fade away. Soon they are no longer in the picture. Why?

The Church structure is built through Paul's ministry. When it comes to the Gentile Church and his ministry to the Gentiles, Paul is an apostle without equal.

Peter, on the other hand, is the apostle to Israel (the Jews), and each of his epistles confirms this fact. When Peter opens his first epistle, he says, "...to the strangers scattered throughout Pontus, Galatia, Cappadocia, Asia, and Bithynia" (1 Pet. 1:1). Who are the strangers scattered abroad? The people of Israel. The Greek word is *diaspora* or "dispersion." This same term is used of Jews today who live outside Israel. So the message of Peter, even in his epistle, is to the Jews.

Paul had a great burden for the Jew and for Israel, but on only one occasion did Paul attempt to minister to the Jews. When he did, he got into trouble. The Holy Spirit told him not to go. He resisted the request of his brethren to return to Jerusalem two times. "In the mouth of two or three witnesses shall every word be established" (2 Cor. 13:1b). The prophets told him not to leave Philippi; even Agabus came down from Caesarea and told him not to go to Jerusalem.

> *And when he was come unto us, he took Paul's girdle, and bound his own hands and feet, and said, Thus saith the Holy Ghost, So shall the Jews at Jerusalem bind the man that owneth this girdle, and shall deliver him into the hands of the Gentiles* (Acts 21:11).

Paul replied, "…I am ready not to be bound only, but also to die at Jerusalem…" (Acts 21:13).

Had it not been for God's grace, he surely would have died. The trip to Jerusalem, his last, was the one time in his ministry as an apostle when he failed to produce one convert. There is no testimony of any fruit ever being born out of that trip. Furthermore, it caused him to experience poor fortune on his trip to Rome, his ultimate destination. Paul might have avoided being emprisoned, shipwrecked, marooned on the Isle of Malta, and finally carried into Rome in bonds.

Still, in all of this there is an important testimony to all of us. Again, I think of the comparison between Paul and Moses. God told Moses to take the rod and speak to the rock to bring forth water; Moses took the rod and smote the rock instead (see Num. 20). It is remarkable that water came out anyhow. Moses did it all wrong, but God did not abandon His responsibility. When Paul did it all wrong, God was not hindered from producing right out of it. God used the occasion to preach the gospel to those on the island and many were brought to Christ. It is evident that Paul holds a special place as the revelator of the dispensation of the grace of God.

Chapter 2

The Gospel According to Paul

What made Paul so unique in his ministry was the gospel that he preached. His gospel was the revelation God had given him. It was the Word of God as Paul received and understood it. Therefore, to reject that word was to reject the word of inspired Scripture.

The Galatians were listening to another voice and another message. "I am amazed that you are so quickly deserting Him who called you by the grace of Christ, for a different gospel" (Gal. 1:6 NAS). This verse is the qualifying point of this epistle. Their call by grace is the way into a new life in Christ—a life in which the believer lives. Under the Old Covenant people were justified by grace also, but they lived in the sphere of law instead of the sphere of grace. This is confirmed in John's Gospel:

And of His fulness have all we received, and grace for grace. For the law was given by

19

Moses, but grace and truth came by Jesus Christ (John 1:16-17).

In the phrase, "And of His fulness have all we received," the idea is that we have received the fullness of grace instead of a portion of grace. The next phrase, "grace for grace" is better understood if translated, "even grace instead of from grace." Here the idea is to exchange the grace of the Old Covenant, which was only a portion, for the grace of the New Covenant, which is full or complete. Through Christ, we have received the fullness of grace instead of a portion of grace. In effect Paul says, "You Galatian believers have been offered more than justification by faith. You have been given the fullness of grace, which is more than the Old Covenant saints realized under the Old Covenant. In reality, by the grace of God, the Kingdom of God is open to you under the New Covenant."

Much has been written on Paul's statement to the Galatians. These writings try to emphasize that the Galatians had fallen from grace. The critics somehow use this to put the Galatian believers on the road to hell. That is not Paul's point at all. He is emphasizing the sphere of grace, the walk of grace, which every believer enjoys through the New Covenant. We can live under legalism or we can live under the grace of God. In either case, we will still go to Heaven. So getting to Heaven is not the issue. On the other hand, we cannot reach maturity under a portion of grace. We can only reach maturity (sonship) under the fullness of grace. As sons, the Spirit of adoption is sent forth into our hearts. So Paul says, "I am amazed that you are so quickly deserting Him who called you, and are now turning to a different gospel."

There is another point to be made here. In Galatians 1:7-9, Paul is concerned with a different gospel. He refers to it as "another gospel." Look for this point in these verses which follow:

> *Which is really not another; only there are some who are disturbing you, and want to distort the gospel of Christ. But even though we, or an angel from heaven, should preach to you a gospel contrary to that which we have preached to you, let him be accursed. As we have said before, so I say again now, if any man is preaching to you a gospel contrary to that which you received, let him be accursed* (Galatians 1:7-9 NAS).

There are two Greek words that can be translated "another," but they have different meanings. One means "another of the same kind" (*allos*), and the second means "another of a different kind" (*heteros*). In verse 6, which reads, "I marvel that ye are so soon removed from Him that called you into the grace of Christ unto another gospel," the Greek word for "another" is *heteros*. Here Paul is referring to a gospel of a different kind, not the gospel he had given them.

Paul goes on to say, "Some have come in and troubled you and perverted the gospel of Christ." They have preached a gospel, but it is not ***the*** gospel. What does the word *gospel* mean? It means "good

21

news." They have given you news that sounds like "good" news, but it is not really *the* good news and it is not the same kind of news you received from Christ."

The Law and the Gospel

Do you hear men and women preach today who call their message "gospel," but really don't preach the gospel at all? The moment you get "me" involved in your gospel message, it is not good news anymore. As soon as you suggest, "God will if you will," it is no longer good news. Our efforts have led us down the bitter trail of failure. It was the law that said, "This do and thou shalt live." This is not the voice of grace. I have heard many who preach a gospel based on the law. That is not good news; it is death. A gospel based on the law is bad news.

How did Jesus answer Nicodemus? "Nicodemus, except a man be born from above, he cannot see the Kingdom of God...Except a man be born of water and of the Spirit, he cannot enter into the Kingdom of God." (See John 3:3,5.) For Nicodemus this was not good news. This was bad news. Why? There was absolutely nothing Nicodemus could do to achieve the Kingdom of God. Still, Nicodemus needed to receive bad news before he could ever receive good news.

What, then, is the purpose of the law? Why must we hear the bad news? The law was put into force to get people to understand that they are lost. A person must know that he is lost before he can be saved. Likewise, only after he knows that he is lost can he lose himself, taking himself completely out of the picture and bringing Christ into full view. Then, the person can see that salvation is of the Lord and that man has nothing to do with redemption. It is God doing for us what we could not and would not do for ourselves. Once we understand, it becomes "good news."

Second Corinthians 11:1-4 points out some of what I have been trying to convey. Paul deals with the same problem in this passage.

> *I wish that you would bear with me in a little foolishness; but indeed you are bearing with me. For I am jealous for you with a godly jealousy; for I betrothed you to one husband, that to Christ I might present you as a pure virgin. But I am afraid, lest as the serpent deceived Eve by his craftiness, your minds should be led astray from the simplicity and purity of devotion to Christ. For if one comes and preaches another Jesus whom we have not preached, or you receive a different spirit which you have not received, or a different gospel which you have not accepted, you bear this beautifully* (2 Corinthians 11:1-4 NAS).

Paul has the same problem with the Corinthian believers that he had with the Galatians. Judaisers had come to Corinth to discredit Paul's gospel message. They told the Corinthians, since Paul was preaching the pure unadulterated grace of God, that he was not really preaching the true gospel. In fact,

23

they claimed that Paul was not an apostle and that he did not have any authority as an apostle. One way they tried to prove their claim was to point out that Paul did not take an offering from them. They said that if he was really an apostle, he would have taken an offering. Paul replied, in essence, "I recognize when I was there that I did not take an offering from you. I surely hope you will forgive me this wrong. The Macedonian believers supplied my want in your lack of supply toward me" (see 2 Cor. 11:9).

In Second Corinthians 11:4 the word *another* might lead you to think this is again the Greek word *heteros*, meaning "another of a different kind." This is not the case. In this verse the Greek word is *allos*, or "another of the same kind." It is the same kind of Jesus, but not the Jesus Paul preached. On the other hand, the Greek word *heteros* is used when Paul refers to "another spirit" and "another gospel."

You may wonder why it is important to look at the meaning behind these Greek words. Paul's use of these specific Greek words is to help us understand that one may preach the same kind of Jesus—one who is loving, redemptive, righteous, merciful, and kind—but who could still be a false Jesus. Paul is saying that this same kind of Jesus that is being preached is not the One (Jesus) he has been preaching. This "other" Jesus requires a contribution from the believer before he can experience the salvation of God. Thus, doing something is a prerequisite for redemption. Unfortunately, as soon as you say, "if you will do," it is another gospel of a different kind. It is the law that says, "This do and thou shalt live."

In this "other" gospel, the believer is back under the law, which corrupts the simplicity of the gospel of Jesus Christ. The ones who preach this "other" gospel are using a subtle tactic to hide their real purpose. They come preaching the same kind of Jesus who delivered us from sin's penalty, but, as they proclaim Jesus, they require a specific act or contribution on our part. They promise liberty, but they are in bondage to self-effort.

Redemption Is Available Without Conditions

Now, I realize that a great deal of what God promises is not without conditions. A classic example is John 15:7: "If you abide in Me, and My words abide in you, ask whatever you wish, and it shall be done for you" (NAS). This promise is obviously conditional. I can ask what I will and get it done as long as I am abiding in the Word. The psalmist put it this way: "And I will walk at liberty [lit., in a wide place], for I seek Thy precepts" (Ps. 119:45 NAS). The good news is a man who hungers and thirsts after the Lord will get what he wants. It is a remarkable and blessed thing to have the privilege of a son. One, who is a son, follows the Lord and God trusts him.

On the other hand, redemption is not conditional. The entire work of salvation and the redemptive work of God requires no participation on an individual's part. It is important for you to understand that I am referring to the believer's position and justification before the Father. You and I have absolutely nothing to do in gaining that position. We cannot add to it and we cannot take from it. It is perfected outside of our realm and we have been brought, by the work of the Father through the Son, into this new realm. It is for our benefit and we are passive recipients of the ongoing work of the Father. Our position in His righteousness is due to His perfect provision. God simply regenerates us and causes us to stand in Him, free from any duties, full of new life.

We learn a lesson from the events described in the Garden of Eden. The serpent, who represents satan, said to the woman, "Eat of the tree of the knowledge of good and evil, and you will be like God." Satan was not promoting wickedness; rather he was promoting righteousness without God. This is the same logic we hear in the message from humanism and legalism today: Determine evil and shun it; determine good and pursue it, and you will be like God. The lie of the deceiver is you can be like God without God.

The ministers of righteousness (see 2 Cor. 11:13-15) were preaching this message: "Do righteously and thereby be approved by God." They sent people to the tree of knowledge of good and evil, which brings death. The letter kills. The real message of *the* good news is that, in Christ, we can eat of the tree of life. This is not following rules; rather, it is developing a relationship. In a relationship with Christ, the rules are irrelevant. The law of ownership works in rules; the law of Love works in relationship.

God has brought us into a salvation that is His work and His alone. It is our privilege to walk in that salvation. Furthermore, it is not realized by the works according to the law, but by accepting His offer through faith in Jesus Christ. In Galatians 3:5 we read, "Does He then, who provides you with the Spirit and works miracles among you, do it by the works of the Law, or by hearing with faith?" (NAS) The obvious response is a loud, "No!" Thus we can see the distinction between the two gospels. The gospel of a different kind says, "This do and thou shalt live." The gospel of Jesus Christ says, "It is finished."

Contrasts in Matthew and Luke

As a further illustration, we might consider the contrast between the Gospels of Matthew and Luke. In Matthew 6:9-13 Jesus instructs His disciples in prayer, a prayer that we know as the Lord's Prayer. Verse 12 says, "And forgive us our debts, as we also have forgiven our debtors" (NAS). Luke 11:4 reads, "And forgive us our sins, for we ourselves also forgive everyone who is indebted to us…" (NAS). Matthew and Luke received what they wrote from the Holy Spirit. However, Matthew's Gospel has a distinctively Jewish emphasis, which relates to the Kingdom of Heaven rather than the Kingdom of God. The Kingdom of Heaven deals with righteousness (or justification), and the Kingdom of God deals with power (or salvation).

Matthew deals with circumstances in the nation of Israel. For example, he writes, "…Do not go in the way of the Gentiles, and do not enter any city of the Samaritans; but rather go to the lost sheep of the house of Israel" (Mt. 10:5-6 NAS). The message is to the people of Israel, who were under a covenant of works. Matthew continues after the Lord's prayer, "For if you forgive men for their transgressions, your heavenly Father will also forgive you. But if you do not forgive men, then your Father will not forgive your transgressions" (Mt. 6:14-15 NAS).

Matthew does not yet consider Luke's perspective, which includes God's plan to provide complete forgiveness. In Luke 11:4, Luke says that we forgive because we have already been forgiven. With that in mind, we can consider what Paul wrote in Ephesians 4:32: "And be kind to one another, tender-hearted, forgiving each other, just as God in Christ also has forgiven you" (NAS).

Why do I forgive under this new economy of God? It's not to get God to forgive me, but because He has already forgiven me. The whole issue of the gospel of grace calls us to respond because of what God has done, not in order to get God to do something. This is the essence of Paul's message to the believers at Ephesus, that we forgive because God, in Christ, has forgiven us. God, in accepting Christ's sacrifice, has acquitted us of all guilt and we stand in the righteousness of God. This is not a pardon. A pardon would set us free, but our guilt would remain with us. This, on the other hand, is a full acquittal. It is as if we were not guilty in the first place.

The kind of Jesus the legalists were preaching looked exactly like the one that Paul was preaching.

The way these legalists got to Him was quite another matter. For example, they might say, "If you will quit hating people, then you will experience the blessings of the forgiving God." How does the good news of the gospel reply to such an attitude? What is my position with the Father? Will God withhold His forgiveness until I quit hating them? What is the answer?

> ...*God was in Christ reconciling the world to Himself, not counting their trespasses against them, and He has committed to us the word of reconciliation* (2 Corinthians 5:19 NAS).

God does not reckon or keep an accounting of my sins anymore. I can approach the Father regardless of my situation, knowing that I am accepted on the basis of the blood of His Son. Whatever the offense, forgiveness begets forgiveness. That is the difference of the good news in Christ. Freely we have received; now freely we give.

Are you without fault? If so, you have no place at the throne of grace. The throne of grace is so named because it is for imperfect people. It is not called the throne of justice. It is the throne of "grace" and not "justice" because it is good news for bad people. Bad people can go to Heaven; good people can go to hell. Jesus did not come to call the righteous, but sinners to repentance. The gospel of Jesus Christ proclaims God's provision for us in an area where we could not help ourselves. Grace is good news for bad people on one condition: that they confess they are bad.

Righteousness based on self-effort and motivated or rooted in fear of rejection serves only to frustrate the grace of God. That is precisely what Paul wrote in Galatians 2:21. He said, "I do not nullify ['frustrate' in the King James Version] the grace of God; for if righteousness comes through the Law, then Christ died needlessly" (NAS).

People come to me from time to time and say, "Brother, I have this problem I have been trying to get rid of for some period of time, but I just cannot. I have done everything I know to do. I have believed God, I've trusted, I've confessed until I'm blue in the face." On they go with all the gimmicks and rituals that they have tried to get rid of their problem. I want to emphasize that confession, verbal confession, can become as big a ritual as any other legalistic rite. Often, I am forced to tell them the truth if it appears that they are playing at confession.

I am absolutely convinced that God wants us free. However, I am concerned about the motivations for a number of us wanting to be free from the problem. Are we remorseful for what we have done wrong? Do we want free out of a concern that we might grieve God? For that matter, are we even concerned that our actions might, in some way, affect our relationship with Him? Rather, we are often more upset because that problem keeps us from looking righteous and spiritual. When I have a problem and people know it, I do not look spiritual. In order to look spiritual, I must get rid of the problem. Therefore, I go through all the procedures hoping God will respond.

If my purpose is to look spiritual or appear righteous before men, or to be numbered among the spiritual giants of God, then God will leave me with the problem. The problem is not bothering Him. As far as He is concerned, the price has been paid. The blood has wiped it out. He will leave me helpless until I discover that my righteousness is not in how well I behave, but in the Lord Jesus Christ alone. I could behave in all the right ways, but God would not accept my behavior apart from Christ. If I do everything right, I still do not measure up. The blood of Jesus Christ is necessary to redeem me from my efforts to do right as well as from my wrong ways.

To begin with, the circumstances of my birth are all wrong. I was born in the first man, Adam, and I was dead in sin. Doing right could not make me better and doing wrong could not make me worse. I was dead in sin. Some of us are in a worse state of decay than others, but dead is dead. In Christ, I have been born again and just as I was a product of birth through Adam, now I am the product of a new birth in Christ. I am now alive in Jesus Christ and in the new life He has given me.

It is His life, not ours, and once again, good deeds cannot make us better and bad deeds cannot make us worse. In the words of Isaiah 64:6, "...and all our righteous deeds are like a filthy garment" (NAS). He has redeemed us from our righteousness as well as our sin.

Scripture helps me understand that I am righteous solely and only because Jesus Christ has paid the price and become my representative in the presence of the Father. When I understand and accept this fact, I must also acknowledge that I am a sinner so the glory might be of God and not of me. Then, I can receive deliverance. If I am not willing to acknowledge my condition, I will remain in bondage lest, being made free from it, I would boast of my righteousness and not His.

Intercessors Identify With the Guilty

Perhaps you have observed that, in Scripture, every man who becomes an intercessor for another was himself a guilty party. Jesus is the classic example of an intercessor. He became what we were in order to bring us where He is. Jesus could not deliver us until He became guilty with us. "He made Him who knew no sin to be sin on our behalf, that we might become the righteousness of God in Him" (2 Cor. 5:21 NAS).

The only way we could be made the righteousness of God is for Him to become sin with us and for us. He did not just have sin laid on Him at the cross. We are wrong if we limit it to that. He became sin. He became the guilty party for every sinful act that you or I ever committed. God saw Him as our sin. The brazen serpent, not the Lamb, symbolizes sin. The Lamb shed blood, which cleansed all from sin. His death, and our justification through His death, was provided for you and me. The blood flowed out of the Lamb, not out of the serpent. Yet Jesus became the serpent, the substitution for sin. God visited death and judgment on Him to deliver you and me from condemnation. Oh, what wonder! He became sin because He had to be identified with who and what we were. He had to be guilty with us in order for us to acquire righteousness from Him.

In the Book of Job God rebuked Job, and then told his three friends to get Job to intercede in prayer for them (see Job 42:7-8). These friends, God said, had not spoken truth concerning Job, but it was Job who received strong rebuke. When God finished rebuking Job, He turned to the three friends and told them to get Job to pray for them and He would forgive them. Here is another case of the intercessor identifying with those who are wrong.

When Abraham was at Gerar, he lied, saying Sarah was his sister. Abimelech, the king of Gerar, took Sarah, but the Lord had "closed fast all the wombs of the household of Abimelech because of Sarah, Abraham's wife" (Gen. 20:18 NAS). The Lord appeared to Abimelech in a dream and warned him about what he was doing. God told Abimelech to restore the woman to Abraham and Abraham would pray for him that he might live. So the king did as he was told, and through Abraham's prayer, the women of his land once again bore children. It is noteworthy that a man whose wife was barren and who was himself guilty of lying, was to pray for children to be born to a nation whose king was guilty through ignorance. This is a good illustration of deliverance from a bondage through the prayer of one who has experienced the same condition.

Remember the words of the prophet Isaiah: "...when Thou shalt make His soul an offering for sin...He hath poured out His soul unto death...and He bare the sin of many, and made intercession for the transgressors" (see Is. 53:10,12).

There are three great imputations in Scripture: (a) the imputation of Adam's sin to the human race, (b) the imputation of the sin of the human race to Christ, and (c) the imputation of the righteousness of Christ to all who believe. It is a remarkable trade, isn't it? The only way God could do it is to have Jesus take my place.

Adam, the first, is a figure of the last Adam (see Rom. 5:14). Adam loved his wife Eve. When she disobeyed God, Adam, not wanting to lose her, thought the only solution was to die with her. I don't mean to diminish the significance of the fall of Adam and, by that fall, the death of the human race. It is important, however, to see the analogy. If Adam was to keep his wife, he must join her. This is precisely what Jesus did for us. Similarly, the law of the harvest is that a corn of wheat must fall to the ground and die—then it will bring forth much fruit. "Christ also loved the church, and gave Himself for it" (Eph. 5:25b).

Second Corinthians 1:3-4 reads,

Blessed be God, even the Father of our Lord Jesus Christ, the Father of mercies, and the God of all comfort; who comforteth us in all our tribulation, that we may be able to comfort them which are in any trouble, by the comfort wherewith we ourselves are comforted of God (2 Corinthians 1:3-4).

Most of our prayers are requests for something we want or think we need. We ask for His will and we trust we will receive of our Father. Nevertheless, our attitude is one of "we may or may not get it," but we hope we do. That is not intercession. In intercession what we ask is granted. Our burden has its origin in God Himself. It has to happen. This kind of ministry in prayer requires us to identify with the circumstances of the one for whom we are praying. This kind of prayer—intercession—is bearing one another's burdens. It fulfills the law of Christ. All intercession is prayer, but not all prayer is intercession.

I cannot be an intercessor for people if I am not willing to identify with them and their problem. I may not have to come where they are, but I must be willing to do so. This is what Moses did when he said, "Yet now, if Thou wilt forgive their sin—; and if not, blot me, I pray Thee, out of Thy book which Thou hast written" (Ex. 32:32). Paul said something similar: "For I could wish that myself were accursed from Christ for my brethren, my kinsmen according to the flesh" (Rom. 9:3). Likewise Adam, without a word, took the fruit of the tree from his wife and thereby became a type of Christ. Jesus Christ "bare our sins in His own body on the tree, that we, being dead to sins, should live unto righteousness: by whose stripes ye were healed" (1 Pet. 2:24).

I emphasize these things to distinguish the true gospel of Jesus Christ from "another" gospel which emanates from those who preach "another" Jesus. As we continue our study of this important message in the Book of Galatians, you will see how crucial it is to our understanding of the truth of redemption and the error of man-centered legalism.

Chapter 3

The Uniqueness of Paul's Gospel

In Chapter 2, I dealt with Paul's concern for believers who might abandon the great gift they had received through the grace of God by accepting "another Jesus" and "another gospel." Paul was determined to expose the process whereby many were being lured back into the web of the law. But this is not what makes Paul's gospel unique, even though it is important to understanding the epistles of Paul and especially the Epistle to the Galatians.

From the Book of Galatians, it is clear that God does not want His people in bondage to a legalized system. It is equally clear that He does want His people to enjoy the "glorious liberty of the children of God" (Rom. 8:21). On the day God gave the law to Moses at Mount Sinai, 3,000 people died in judgment. On the day God sent the Holy Spirit to make us sons of God, 3,000 people were saved. What a marvelous contrast!

Obedience of Faith

Who was declared the Son of God with power by the resurrection from the dead, according to the spirit of holiness, Jesus Christ our Lord, through whom we have received grace and apostleship to bring about the obedience of faith among all the Gentiles, for His name's sake (Romans 1:4-5 NAS).

Now to Him who is able to establish you according to my gospel and the preaching of Jesus Christ, according to the revelation of the mystery which has been kept secret for long ages past, but now is manifested, and by the Scriptures of the prophets, according to the commandment of the eternal God, has been made known to all the nations, leading to obedience of faith (Romans 16:25-26 NAS).

In these two passages from the Book of Romans the emphasis is on the phrase "obedience of faith." The core of Paul's gospel, a theme that runs through his epistles, is obedience of faith. Paul is not concerned with obedience to the law, because, for Paul, a walk of faith is the obvious goal. Even more to the point, the issue for Paul is obedience that emanates from and is the product of faith. This is in direct contrast to obedience that is demanded by a system of law. Paul wrote,

For the love of Christ controls us, having concluded this, that one died for all, therefore all

died; and He died for all, that they who live should no longer live for themselves, but for Him who died and rose again on their behalf (2 Corinthians 5:14-15 NAS).

In presenting Paul's gospel, I am aware that you might ask, "Is Paul's gospel different from any other New Testament writing?" There is as much uniqueness about Paul's gospel as there is with his apostleship. He makes reference to "my gospel" in Romans 2:16: "In the day when God shall judge the secrets of men by Jesus Christ according to my gospel."

Paul stands out from the rest of the disciples who carried the ministry of the resurrection of Jesus Christ. The message Paul brought to the Church is the basis of the believer's reward at the judgment seat of Christ (see 1 Cor. 3:10-15). Paul, not the other apostles, is the messenger to the Body of Christ and, as its messenger, outlines its judgment and reward. For Paul to use the expression "my gospel" would be the height of arrogance if there was not something unique in his message. This uniqueness appears in the second and sixteenth chapters of Romans where he emphasizes obedience and reward. Sandwiched between these two basic and important points, lies the balance of Paul's message.

The Salvation of God

The Book of Romans is the foundational treatise of Paul's gospel; it presents the whole concept of justification by faith. "I am under obligation both to

Greeks and to barbarians, both to the wise and to the foolish. Thus, for my part, I am eager to preach the gospel to you also who are in Rome" (Rom. 1:14-15 NAS). These verses, when read in light of verse 8, bring up an interesting point: "First, I thank my God through Jesus Christ for you all, because your faith is being proclaimed throughout the whole world" (Rom. 1:8 NAS). If their faith is proclaimed throughout the whole world, it is reasonable to ask, "Why does the apostle Paul want to come and preach the gospel to those who are at Rome?" He told the Corinthian believers that his desire was to preach Christ where He had not been named and not to build on another man's foundation. Why is Paul coming to preach to the Romans if they are already a body of believers whose faith is announced in all the world? It is because he wants to go beyond or to expand what they have already received.

The gospel begins with justification through faith, but the end of the gospel is the salvation of God. The Roman believers had not yet experienced the salvation of God because this salvation is predicated on the resurrection of Jesus Christ from the dead. This is the core of Paul's gospel as he states in Romans 1:4: "Who was declared the Son of God with power by the resurrection from the dead, according to the spirit of holiness, Jesus Christ our Lord" (NAS). Paul's gospel is based upon the power of the resurrection. The Holy Spirit could not be poured out until Jesus was raised from the dead and glorified at the right hand of the Father.

"He who believes in Me, as the Scripture said, 'From his innermost being shall flow rivers of living water.' " But this He spoke of the Spirit, whom those who believed in Him were to receive; for the Spirit was not yet given, because Jesus was not yet glorified (John 7:38-39 NAS).

Peter's words confirm this as he speaks right after these events take place:

Therefore having been exalted to the right hand of God, and having received from the Father the promise of the Holy Spirit, He has poured forth this which you both see and hear (Acts 2:33 NAS).

Jesus is raised from the dead "because of our justification" (see Rom. 4:25 NAS). Once we were justified by His blood, Christ was raised again from the dead and was seated at the right hand of the Father in glory. Then, He sent forth the Holy Spirit. This progression brings us from justification by faith into the salvation of God.

The Old Testament saints knew what it was to be justified by faith. Abraham believed God and he was declared righteous on the basis of his belief (see Jas. 2:23). Noah, David, Enoch—all these were accepted by God through their faith. "These all died in faith, not having received the promises, but having seen them afar off were assured of them..." (Heb. 11:13 NKJ). What is the distinction between what they had received and what we have received? They knew

41

what it was like to be established in righteousness, but we know what it is like to be established in the power of God, which is the salvation of God.

In Luke 1:77, Zacharias prophesied that John the Baptist would "give knowledge of salvation unto His people by the remission of their sins." Under the Old Covenant sin was not removed, but simply covered. That was the concept of atonement in the Old Covenant. In the New Covenant, Jesus came that sin might be removed or taken "away from" the believer in Christ.

This atonement was what the saints of past ages anticipated and desired. In writing his Gospel, it was appropriate for Matthew to address his message with emphasis on Israel and the advent of the Kingdom of Heaven. The Kingdom of Heaven deals with righteousness and, more specifically, the absolute righteousness of God imputed to the believer. The Kingdom of Heaven began with the tearing of the veil in the temple, which laid open the entrance to the Holy of Holies. By the blood of Jesus, we have free access to God's throne.

The Kingdom of God is now open as a result of that righteousness, and within that Kingdom is power and authority. As Zacharias said, salvation is come because of remission. A close and dear friend of mine made it clear when he said, "The Kingdom of Heaven is to be like Jesus on earth—the Kingdom of God is to be like Christ in Heaven."

Matthew is the only writer that uses the expression, "Kingdom of Heaven." I think it is because he was led by the Spirit to deal with the advent of the New Covenant. Even the parables he includes in his Gospel emphasize the distinction between those who stand in God's righteousness and those who do not. For example, Matthew 5:20 reads, "...unless your righteousness exceeds the righteousness of the scribes and Pharisees, you will by no means enter the kingdom of heaven" (NKJ). This is typical of his theme.

One exception to Matthew's theme can be found in chapter 12. In this section he gives a foretaste of the Kingdom of God. He tells us that Jesus was being questioned by the Pharisees who claimed He was casting out demons by the prince or ruler of demons, Beelzebub. Jesus replied to the Pharisees by saying, "But if I cast out demons by the Spirit of God, surely the kingdom of God has come upon you" (Mt. 12:28 NKJ). Under the law of the Old Testament, they stoned a man who was demon-possessed. With the advent of the Kingdom of God, Jesus saved the man and cast out the demon. The Kingdom of Heaven began when the veil was removed and the Most Holy Place exposed. The Kingdom of God began with the outpouring of the Holy Spirit on the Day of Pentecost.

This is the salvation that was prophesied by the prophet Zechariah. "...Behold, your King is coming to you; He is just and having salvation..." (Zech. 9:9 NKJ). The Kingdom of God is the power of God, which brings the salvation of God to the people of God. The psalmist put it plainly: "But the salvation of the righteous is from the Lord" (Ps. 37:39 NKJ).

Paul says in Romas 1:15-16 (NAS):

Thus, for my part, I am eager to preach the gospel to you also who are in Rome. [I will remind you that *gospel* means "good news".] *For I am not ashamed of the gospel, for it is the power of God for salvation to everyone who believes....*

The gospel is not for justification, sanctification, or reconciliation. The gospel is for salvation. Some may say, "I thought all those words meant the same thing." No, they do not mean the same thing at all. Justification is right standing before God; sanctification is separation unto God; and reconciliation is right relationship with God—but salvation is the life of God.

For I am not ashamed of the gospel, for it is the power of God for salvation to everyone who believes [not who works], *to the Jew first and also to the Greek. For in it the righteousness of God is revealed from faith to faith; as it is written, "But the righteous man shall live by faith"* (Romans 1:16-17 NAS).

God's Righteousness Versus Man's Righteousness

Romans 1:17 emphasizes two important truths. First, Paul tells us that it is God's righteousness that is revealed. How is that distinct from righteousness under the law? Under the law it was my righteousness that was revealed. Deuteronomy 6:25 reads, "And it shall be our righteousness, if we observe to do all these commandments before the Lord our God, as He hath commanded us."

In Philippians Paul tells us how he views his life and how he wants to be found in Christ.

> *But whatever things were gain to me, those things I have counted as loss for the sake of Christ. ... And may be found in Him, not having a righteousness of my own derived from the Law, but that which is through faith in Christ, the righteousness which comes from God on the basis of faith* (Phil. 3:7,9 NAS).

Righteousness through the law is righteousness that I get credit for achieving. It draws attention to me, not to God. Under the law my life continues because I follow or do right according to the law ("this do and thou shalt live"). Therefore if I am enjoying a life of blessing, it is because I am doing well. The glory is mine and not God's. Paul says that the gospel of the salvation of God is the righteousness of God revealed. This is righteousness imputed to me on the basis of the finished work of Jesus Christ.

The second truth from Romans 1:17 that I want to emphasize is that faith begins as a seed and matures into the full fruit. It is from "faith to faith." From the beginning, faith is a faith in the process of maturing from justifying faith to saving faith. The prophet Habakkuk tells us, "...but the just shall live by his faith" (Hab. 2:4). This same phrase occurs in three New Testament epistles, but each places a different emphasis on faith. In Hebrews 10:38 the just endure in hope by faith (see also Heb. 11:1). In Galatians 3:11 the just live by faith in liberty as sons of God. In Romans 1:17 the just receive the salvation of God by faith. In Hebrews, I find I can come into rest by faith; in Galatians, I come into liberty by faith; in Romans, I come into salvation by faith.

This is the basic view of Paul's message, as given to him by the Spirit, throughout the whole of his 14 epistles: *The justified are coming into salvation.* Those who live by faith are realizing what true liberty is, and those who walk by faith will come into rest.

Chapter 4

Salvation—the Heart of Paul's Message

In the previous chapter we introduced the salvation of God as the heart of Paul's message. All too often it is confused with or considered the same as justification. In examining this point more fully, you will understand the need for and the severity of Paul's warnings and condemnation of those perverting his gospel message. Paul's concern was so great that he established a severe penalty for anyone who would pervert his gospel.

In his letter to the Romans, Paul tells us that Jesus "was delivered up because of our offenses, and was raised because of our justification" (Rom. 4:25 NKJ). Note the phrase, "because of our offenses [transgressions]." He shed His blood and died because we were transgressors. The same usage is in the phrase "raised because of our justification." He was not raised from the dead in order to justify us, but because we were already justified by His blood. He bought and paid for our righteousness on the cross. Now, in His resurrection He has given us His life. It is His blood that has justified us; it is His resurrection that saves us.

His justifying work was all that was necessary to take us to Heaven, but with His resurrection, His life has brought Heaven to us as a gift through the indwelling Holy Spirit. This is salvation. Salvation is not only peace with God—it is the peace of God.

Peace With God

Beginning in Romans 5, Paul uses a particular style by introducing a number of his statements with the word *therefore* followed by a discourse on the point he is making. "Therefore being justified by faith, we have peace with God through our Lord Jesus Christ" (Rom. 5:1). This first "therefore" begins an interesting progression in Paul's letters that starts with "peace with," changes to "peace from" and then becomes "the peace of God." In this first verse the phrase "peace with God" is a judicial ruling declaring the fact of reconciliation. God and man are no longer at war. When I believe God, my warfare ceases and I am at peace with Him.

Judicial peace, however, does not necessarily mean that I experience peace personally and emotionally. Personal and emotional peace is realized by seeing, through faith, what grace has provided through Jesus Christ and then resting in His finished work. "By whom also we have access [Paul's way of saying that Jesus is the Door] by faith into this grace wherein we stand, and rejoice in hope of the glory of God" (Rom 5:2).

"Much more then, being now justified by His blood, we shall be saved from wrath through Him" (Rom 5:9). How is that accomplished? Verse 10 explains: "For if, when we were enemies, we were reconciled to God by the death of His Son, much more, being reconciled, we shall be saved by His life." It does not say we receive salvation through His "death." The justification of the believer is by His blood; reconciliation is by His death; and salvation is by His life.

Justification

Justification, simply defined, is a judicial act of God whereby the believing sinner is counted as righteous in the court of Heaven. All guilt is dissolved and God finds nothing wrong with that individual. He is not pardoned; he is acquitted.

There are a number of illustrations of a guilty person who, deserving the death penalty, instead receives a pardon from the governor at the last moment and gets his freedom instead. This makes for an exciting end to a movie, but that is not what justification is all about. If you pardon a person, he goes free—but you leave him with his guilt. When a person is acquitted, it is as if he were not guilty in the first place. The forgiven believer, standing in the presence of God, stands without sin—past, present, or future.

This truth seems to be difficult for believers to understand. We believe that Jesus has forgiven us of all the sins we committed prior to the time we were saved. We can even believe He has forgiven all of our sins up to the present time. (See First John 1:9, a verse we often confess.) But most of us have a hard time with the sins we have not yet committed. Oh, we of little faith!

If Jesus could die for me 2,000 years before I was born and take care of all the sins that I might commit from birth to the point of justification, surely He can forgive sins I have not yet committed. If He could see all of that before it happened, He has surely seen all that I have not yet thought of or done. He has, indeed, forgiven me those sins as well. All of the sins I have not yet committed were also imputed to Jesus Christ on the cross. He has forgiven us all trespasses. That is good news and that is why it is called "gospel."

The real issue facing the believer is whether or not he will believe it. One of the old hymns says, "Once for all, Oh sinner receive it, once for all, Oh brother believe it" ("Once for All," P.P. Bliss). I get the distinct impression that the songwriter recognized the problem many now face. We do have a difficult time believing that God has forgiven all our trespasses. We also have a hard time believing we have been "justified from all things, from which ye could not be justified by the law of Moses" (Acts 13:39b).

Justification, then, is the position in which the believer stands. They understood that in the Church at Rome. What they did not recognize was that, as a result of their standing with God and of the life of Jesus Christ that was imparted to them, they did not have to wait to live in the salvation of God. Most of us do not live in God's salvation. We do not live in the peace of God. We are still afraid that when we do something wrong, God gets angry with us and we lose our standing. Justification is altogether by blood and has nothing to do with how we behave. We will never be any more righteous than the blood of Christ has made us.

Imputed Death

The story of Jonah is a good illustration of this next point. Jonah tried to escape the responsibility God had called him to accept by boarding a boat bound for Tarshish. On the voyage he was identified as the one who was guilty of causing the storm that threatened the ship and the crew. The crew said to Jonah, "What should we do to you that the sea may become calm for us?" Jonah said, "Pick me up and throw me into the sea. Then the sea will become calm for you." (See Jonah 1:11-12.)

Have you ever asked yourself why Jonah did not just jump overboard? It was because his death had to be their fault. If he had jumped overboard, he would have died—but so would they. His death had to be imputed to them. The death of Christ must, of necessity, be imputed to us. His death had to be our fault.

51

Jesus did not commit suicide; He died at the hands of sinful man. Jesus cites the record of Jonah as a type of His death, burial, and resurrection (see Mt. 12:39-40). If we did not die in Christ, then we cannot be raised in Him. But His death is a substitute for our death in order that His resurrection life might be our life as well.

Jonah further illustrates the good news of a finished work. When Jonah told the mariners to throw him overboard, they determined not to do so. Rather, they rowed hard to bring the boat to land. They had already thrown the cargo into the sea to lighten the load. So, they rowed the harder to keep from having to throw Jonah out of the boat.

Do you see the lesson, now that you can see Jonah as a type of Christ? Like the seaman who chose to row harder rather than cast Jonah to his death, we often turn to self-effort rather than turning fully to the death of Christ for our deliverance. In order to change, we may start by removing self-effort from our lives. We stop doing first one thing and then another. We stop going here and then we stop going there. A change of life style may be desirable, but self-depravation does not bring deliverance—and neither does additional self-effort. We are also inclined to believe increased spiritual activity brings the peace we long for, but this too is not the case. Rowing harder in our walk with the Lord is a contradiction. It will not help us to grow in grace. Only submission to the death of Christ and His finished work brings the work of the cross and the power of the resurrection into our lives. God offers a message of peace to us, and we turn it into a message of bondage. Having begun in the Spirit, we constantly turn to the flesh for perfection.

New Birth

Romans 5:10 is the great transition point for Paul's thesis in this book. "For if while we were enemies, we were reconciled to God through the death of His Son, much more, having been reconciled, we shall be saved by [in] His life" (NAS). From this point on, Paul deals with issues that relate to the salvation of God and especially to how we walk in that salvation. For example, Romans 6 considers the new birth. The new birth is a result of the New Covenant work of Christ and is experienced through the outpouring of the person of the Holy Spirit. Since no one in the Old Testament had experienced the new birth, Paul outlines the elements and process of the born-again experience.

The opportunity for the new birth experience began on the Day of Pentecost. To be born again is to be raised from the dead. Jesus is the firstborn from the dead, the firstborn among many brethren (see Col. 1:18; Rom. 8:29). New birth is not forgiveness. New birth is resurrection life.

Baptized Into Christ

Or do you not know that all of us who have been baptized into Christ Jesus have been baptized into His death? Therefore we have been buried with Him through baptism into death, in order that as Christ was raised from the dead through the glory of the Father, so we too might walk in newness of life (Romans 6:3-4 NAS).

This is the same baptism (placing into) that Paul speaks of in First Corinthians 12:13. It is by the Holy Spirit that we are joined into Christ's death and burial, and then raised in His life. As many as were baptized or "joined in union" with Jesus Christ, were "joined in union" with His death. Here begins the treatise on the new birth that is the foundation for the message which our Lord gave to this great apostle.

For if we have become united with Him in the likeness of His death, certainly we shall be also in the likeness of His resurrection, knowing this, that our old self was crucified with Him, that our body of sin might be done away with, that we should no longer be slaves to sin; for he who has died is freed from sin (Romans 6:5-7 NAS).

You died in Christ. If you know you are dead with Him, then, "...consider yourselves to be dead to sin, but alive to God in Christ Jesus. Therefore do not let sin reign in your mortal body that you should obey its lusts" (Rom. 6:11-12 NAS). Note the word *consider* (in verse 11). The King James Version translates it as "reckon." The words *consider*, *reckon*, and *impute* are all renderings of the same Greek word that simply means to "put to the account of." God has imputed His death to you; now you must impute that death to yourself.

The Problem of Righteousness

To examine this issue we turn to Romans 7. "For I know that nothing good dwells in me, that is, in my flesh..." (Rom 7:18 NAS). Do we agree with this statement? Not really. We want to believe that there is still some good thing in us, so we try to prove it by making it happen. Remember, "all our righteousnesses are as filthy rags" (Is. 64:6). The problem that God has with us is not our sin. We want to rid ourselves of our sins. It is our righteousness that gets in the way. As long as I can recommend myself to God in any area, I am unacceptable for the purposes of God. But when I finally decide to agree with God and confess that no good thing is in me, then I am in a position for God to do something for me and through me.

"For the good that I wish, I do not do; but I practice the very evil that I do not wish. But if I am doing the very thing I do not wish, I am no longer the one doing it, but sin which dwells in me" (Rom. 7:19-20 NAS). Again, do you see the separation that Paul has drawn between sin and action? You say, "But, I did it!" You are missing the point. You have died to that old man and God has separated you from him and all his sins, even those sins not yet done. Since God has separated you from sin, Paul says that it is no longer you who sins. Rather, it is the nature of sin that works in your body.

This is the body of sin that died with Him on the cross. He has separated you by death from the old man and raised you to life as a new man. The new man stands in the righteousness of God through Jesus Christ. The deeds of the old man can in no way affect your position before God. You are acquitted of all the things you could not receive justification for through the law of Moses (see Acts 13:39). Did you ever say of someone, "I do not understand how God can bless that person. His behavior is so intolerable." The answer is that God can bless and use that individual because he is justified by the blood and he is being saved by the power of the resurrection of Jesus Christ.

God is not imputing to believers their trespasses. Many of us who have these thoughts should remember that sin in our eyes is relative. That is to say, we look at some sin as tolerable and some as intolerable. If a person's behavior does not violate our code of conduct, we are comfortable when the Lord uses him. Actually, He uses us in spite of who we are and what we have done, not because of who we are and what we have done. Psalm 130:3 makes this clear: "If You, Lord, should mark iniquities, O Lord, who could stand?" (NKJ)

Commitment

This new relationship we have with the Father, through Christ, is extremely important. Second

Corinthians 5 gives us insight into this subject. "For the love of Christ controls us, having concluded this, that one died for all, therefore all died" (2 Cor. 5:14 NAS). So you are either dead in sin or you are dead to sin, one or the other. "And He died for all, that they who live should no longer live for themselves, but for Him who died and rose again on their behalf" (2 Cor. 5:15 NAS). The plea in this verse is based on our relationship.

You may say, "Well, if I am dead in Christ and sin is no longer imputed to me or not reckoned to me, what is my responsibility?" Paul just told you. If Jesus died for you, then you must live to and for Him. What is your commitment to be? It is not to the deeds of righteousness, but to Him. He will look after all the deeds of righteousness when the believer is *fully surrendered to Him.*

> *Therefore from now on we recognize no man according to the flesh* [that is, according to the carnal ability]; *even though we have known Christ according to the flesh, yet now we know Him thus no longer* (2 Corinthians 5:16 NAS).

Paul knew the Messiah, as the Scriptures taught Him. That was carnal knowledge based on a carnal system (see Heb. 7:16). Many believers live in the realm of carnal understanding about Christ. They could write a long doctrinal treatise on Christology. But when it comes to knowing Him personally and intimately, in a relationship that guides one down the path of righteousness, that is another matter.

"Therefore if any man is in Christ, he is a new creature; the old things passed away; behold, new things have come. Now all these things are from God..." (2 Cor. 5:17-18 NAS).

Is everything in you of God? That is what Paul said. Perhaps you are thinking, "Well, not everything that comes out of me is of God!" You are missing the point. God has given you a new relationship with Him and a new imputation from Him. He counts you as righteous. Much of what you and I do is out of the sin that works in our members, in our body. He wants you to see yourself through the cross, separated from the body of sin in His sight.

Sin and Trespass

"...God was in Christ reconciling the world to Himself, not counting their trespasses against them..." (2 Cor. 5:19 NAS). Notice Paul said "trespasses" and not "sins." There is a big difference between sin and trespass. You can commit a sin and not know it. Sin is simply coming short of the appointed mark or coming short of the glory of God (see Rom. 3:23). The word *trespass*, however, means to proceed beyond a known line, to violate a known regulation or stipulation. It means to disobey a commandment willfully.

At the cross, "God was in Christ reconciling the world unto Himself, not counting their trespasses against them." So God did not even impute to you what you did when you knew you ought not do it. That is good news! "He made Him who knew no sin to be sin on our behalf, that we might become the righteousness of God in Him" (2 Cor. 5:21 NAS). Keep in mind we are not addressing our walk or our continuing growth in Christ, but rather our position before the Father through Christ Jesus.

Motivation to Obedience

If we examine our propensity to sin, we can discover what might turn us to a more holy walk. I have committed a sin and am deeply grieved at having done so. But is my confession of sin and my sorrow for my action enough to motivate me to do right? The answer is, "No!" Actually, it will bring about utter discouragement. A perfect example always brings one under the heel of condemnation. Always! For example, I can read of men who have been preaching for years and I end up asking myself, "Why am I in the ministry?" Ask the average pianist if listening to an accomplished professional will improve his or her own playing. Perfect example does not motivate us to improvement—it destroys us.

Often we hear that we are supposed to observe Jesus and do what He did. That sounds like a good program. The only problem is, it does not work. That is what we had under the law. The law was the manifestation of the character of God and of Christ. We have tried it, have we not? It did not work. So is it wise to return to a system that could not bring peace? That is precisely what Paul saw as a problem with the believers in Galatia. Having begun their walk in the Spirit, they now were turning back to the law to overcome the flesh and walk in maturity. It is vanity, empty and void of success.

The law could not move me to righteousness and a sorrowful heart could not move me to righteousness. So what does move me to do righteously and sin not? The goodness of God leads me to repentance (see Rom. 2:4). God has done wonderfully in my behalf and the better I understand this, the more I respond to Him in obedience. Thus growing in grace is understanding our great need of Him, while growing in knowledge is understanding His great provision for us. The more we grow, the more we obey.

The Old Man and the Flesh

We can increase our understanding by giving some attention to "the old man." This phrase only occurs three times in the New Testament epistles: once each in Romans, in Colossians, and in Ephesians. Each time it occurs, it is always in the passive tense, never in the active tense. The old man has been crucified. It is a finished work, a finished crucifixion. He is dead and stays that way. You may rightly ask, "Then why am I having so much trouble with control?" It is the flesh. The flesh and the old man are not the same thing. If only the evangelicals could learn this! Over and over again I hear preachers on Christian radio preaching that we have to crucify the old man. The old man is already crucified—dead and buried! The flesh is the problem.

The old man, before he was the "old man," had educated the mind of the believer to walk in his ways. The appetites of the body of sin had so established our value system that those appetites took dominion over our every action, if permitted to do so. Therefore, a conflict is created between our spirit wanting to obey God and our body being drawn to do the deeds of the flesh. This is why Paul tells the believers in Rome to renew their minds. I see my mind renewed when I present my body as a living sacrifice as Paul urged.

> *I urge you therefore, brethren, by the mercies of God, to present your bodies a living and holy sacrifice, acceptable to God, which is your spiritual service of worship. And do not be conformed to this world, but be transformed by the renewing of your mind, that you may prove what the will of God is, that which is good and acceptable and perfect* (Romans 12:1-2 NAS).

It is worth noting that "be transformed" and "be conformed" are verbs in the passive sense. If I do not present my body, then I will be conformed to this world. If I do present my body, then I will be transformed and ultimately conformed to the image of Jesus Christ (see Rom. 8:29). By presenting my body, I find a source outside of myself doing the work of transformation. So we were asked to present our body, not our life to the Lord. This is because our body is the vehicle in which the Spirit wishes to move. We lost our life at Calvary, and it is now hid with Christ in God. "And if Christ is in you, though

61

the body is dead because of sin, yet the spirit is alive because of righteousness" (Rom. 8:10 NAS).

The desire to obey comes from having been justified. The ability to obey comes from the indwelling of the Spirit, who is the life of Jesus Christ. The desire to obey is evidence that we are righteous in Christ. The ability to obey is the experience of the salvation of God. It is the love of Christ within us that precipitates deeds of righteousness. When we do what we want to do and not what we feel like doing, that is practical righteousness. Feelings arise from our body of sin, but the desire to obey arises from our redeemed spirit. We may have severe and complicated demands from within that want to fulfill our view of righteousness, but God's requirements are simple and come from the heart. "For this is the love of God, that we keep His commandments: and His commandments are not grievous" (1 Jn. 5:3). Micah 6:8 reads, "He hath shewed thee, O man, what is good; and what doth the Lord require of thee, but to do justly, and to love mercy, and to walk humbly with thy God?"

In Matthew 11 Jesus urges us to take upon us His burden. Ours is heavy, but His is light. In First Peter 5 we are called to cast all our care on Christ, for He cares for us. Carrying the weight of failure will destroy the strongest of Christians. Can we roll that failure on Him? Can we say, "Okay, Lord, I did it, but it was not me. It was sin that dwells in me"? Yes, we can and we must. This is a remarkable—yes, Divine—example of grace!

Some may question these truths, claiming they give people a license to sin. Actually, the believer who knows and experiences the indwelling life of Jesus Christ respects the gift God has given him or her and reacts to His great love by avoiding sin. The motivation is the love of Christ. As Paul wrote, "For the grace of God has appeared, bringing salvation to all men, instructing us to deny ungodliness and worldly desires and to live sensibly, righteously and godly in the present age" (Tit. 2:11-12 NAS). The law works from without; grace works from within. The nature of the New Covenant is inward life, not outward command.

> ..."I will put My law within them, and on their heart I will write it; and I will be their God, and they shall be My people. And they shall not teach again, each man his neighbor and each man his brother, saying, 'Know the Lord,' for they shall all know Me, from the least of them to the greatest of them," declares the Lord... (Jeremiah 31:33-34 NAS).

An unknown poet said it well:

> Run and work, the law demands;
> But gives me neither feet nor hands.
> But sweeter truth the gospel brings;
> It bids me fly and gives me wings.

Chapter 5

Concepts and Terms Associated With the New Birth

Often pastors and teachers will use a word or a phrase over and over again and assume their hearers understand what they are trying to convey. Just as often there is a degree of confusion with these words and phrases. I believe it would be useful to take time to provide a brief definition of important terms associated with the new birth.

Justification: Justification is such an important term, I provided a complete discussion of this term in Chapter 4. I will not take the time to go over it again. I only want to remind you that the justified believer is one who has, through God's judicial decree, been declared righteous in the court of Heaven.

Salvation: This word is used to express the Old Testament concept for "deliverance," or being made safe from harm (see Rom. 10:13; Joel 2:32). Salvation in the Old Testament was always temporal and related to a specific incident where a person or the nation needed help to escape harm or death. King David sought salvation or deliverance from his enemies (see Ps. 35:1-3). The salvation of God we experience under the New Covenant was not available to the Old Testament saints. Salvation, as it comes to us from God, is spiritual and personal. He saves us first from ourselves. We are delivered from our old, carnal man, from the devil, and from the world.

The same Greek word translated "salvation" is also used in connection with physical healing (see Mk. 6:56). Broadly speaking, salvation refers to the wholeness of God. There is a trinity of evil within man: the lust of the flesh, the lust of the eyes, and the pride of life. Similarly, there is a trinity of evil outside of man: the world, the flesh, and the devil. We have been delivered from the lust of the flesh, the lust of the eyes, and the pride of life which plagued us from within. This deliverance comes as the old man is crucified with Christ. Paul says, "...our old self was crucified with Him, that our body of sin might be done away with, that we should no longer be slaves to sin" (Rom. 6:6 NAS). We have been delivered from the trinity of evil without through "the blood of the Lamb, and by the word of [our] testimony" (Rev. 12:11).

Regeneration: To regenerate is to put new life into something. There was life, but life ceased. Now life has been restored and that which is dead is alive once again. Before Adam sinned, he was alive with God in the Garden. Then he disobeyed God, and life as he knew it ceased. Life was restored when Jesus, the last Adam, restored man's relationship with God. Through the first man, Adam, sin came into the world, and death by sin. In the last Adam, life came into the world, and righteousness by that life.

Regeneration is Paul's term for the new birth. It is "the washing of regeneration, and renewing of the Holy Ghost" (Tit. 3:5b). We have been raised from the dead, and the life of God has returned to us. "Even when we were dead in our transgressions, [God] made us alive together with Christ (by grace you have been saved)" (Eph. 2:5 NAS). We were dead in sin, but now we are raised to life in the person of Christ. There is no regeneration, no life apart from Him.

Sanctification: The word *sanctification* enjoys a variety of interpretations. The most simple definition is "set apart." The same root word is also translated "holy," and they all mean the same thing. This Greek word was not exclusive to Christianity, nor was it reserved for godly purposes. It was also used to describe temple prostitutes and brothels that were "set apart." The English word *saint* is by definition "one who has been sanctified or made holy." So in that sense, anyone who is "set apart" for a specific purpose can be called a "saint," as were certain Corinthians who worshiped the goddess of fertility.

In using this term Paul is saying, in effect, "If the devil has his set-apart ones, then God has those who are set apart to Him." The Hebrew equivalent to the Greek word was used of anything or anyone devoted to any kind of god. When it is applied to a person or a thing, it means he or she has been "separated to and for the use of" the god or God. First Thessalonians 1:9 reads, "...you turned to God from idols to serve a living and true God" (NAS). The believer has not just turned from the world into a kind of vacuum, but has turned to God from the world.

God is holy and "thus you are to be holy to Me, for I the Lord am holy" (Lev. 20:26a NAS). In what way is God holy? The first thing we read into the words *sanctify*, *holy*, or *saint* is righteousness, but this verse says nothing about God being righteous. God is holy because He is set apart from all His creation. His grand and glorious Person is separate from sinful man.

God created the tabernacle to demonstrate the fact that He is set apart. In the tabernacle, anyone who had a sacrifice could enter the Outer Court, but only the priests could come into the Holy Place. This was further divided and the final room was called the Most Holy Place. Once a year the high priest alone could enter this area, which was the dwelling place of God, sanctified (set apart) unto Him.

Paul also refers to the believer as the temple or tabernacle of God (see 1 Cor. 3:16; 6:19). In First Thessalonians 5:22-23 he tells the believer, "Abstain from all appearance of evil. And the very God of peace sanctify you wholly; and I pray God your whole spirit and soul and body be preserved blameless unto the coming of our Lord Jesus Christ." Your spirit is sanctified because the Spirit of Christ dwells there. Your soul is being sanctified because of the renewing of your mind. Your body is sanctified because of the impending resurrection.

Each of these three areas is in a different degree of sanctification, which is dictated by their proximity to the world. It is not a matter of less importance; rather, it is a matter of less proximity to Him who is absolutely holy. My spirit is sanctified from the defilement of this world; my soul is being sanctified from the defilement of this world, and my body will be sanctified from the defilement of this world.

Another way to state it is to say this: "I am sanctified, positionally in spirit, practically in soul, and ultimately in body." Jesus, by contrast, is perfect in all areas. The Epistle to the Hebrews confirms this in saying He is "holy, innocent, undefiled, separated from sinners..." (Heb. 7:26 NAS). Paul writes to the Corinthians: "...to those who have been sanctified in Christ Jesus, saints by calling..." (1 Cor. 1:2 NAS). In that one verse, both the verb and the noun forms of holy are used. This means they are positionally saints and are experientially being sanctified. Having established this fact, Paul begins to admonish them with regard to their walk. They did not look holy, they did not act holy, but they were holy because of their position in Christ. Thus, Paul will spend the rest of this epistle addressing the practical application of their position. What Paul is saying is, "Stop behaving like what you are not and start behaving like what you are."

When I say that believers are holy, that does not insure that they are walking in righteousness. Husbands who are lost are referred to as holy because of their Christian wives. It is through the believing spouse that the home and children are made holy (see 1 Cor. 7:14). Those who are redeemed by His blood are made holy so they can be examples of righteous living. We do not become righteous to be holy—we become holy to be righteous.

If we are not set apart from the world, we will not walk in practical righteousness. So after we have been set apart by God for His use, we are responsible to continue in holiness. "For this is the will of God, even your sanctification, that ye should abstain from..." (1 Thess. 4:3). He has, first of all, sanctified us. Then He begins to perfect our holiness. Paul put it this way to the Corinthians: "Having therefore these promises, dearly beloved, let us cleanse ourselves from all filthiness of the flesh and spirit, perfecting holiness in the fear of God" (2 Cor. 7:1).

Ransom and Redemption: It will be helpful to contrast the Old Testament term *ransom* with the word *redemption*. In a very broad view, ransom was what was observed in the Old Testament, while redemption is available in the New Testament because of the finished work of the cross. Ransom is the price paid. Redemption is deliverance from the debt. You can pay a ransom and not receive back the person who is in bondage. God has paid our ransom for our bondage to sin and the world and, by the power of the resurrection, brought about our redemption. It is important that we do not confuse these two terms.

In leaving Egypt, Israel's ransom was paid when the lamb was slain at the Passover, but redemption was not realized until they crossed the Red Sea. Practical deliverance was finally realized when the Israelites went into the land of Canaan, but positional deliverance took place when they crossed the Red Sea. This is a good picture of the salvation of God, or the power of God, working in the redeemed.

Reconciliation: There are two aspects of "reconciliation" we need to consider. In Romans 5:10, we read, "For if, when we were enemies, we were reconciled to God by the death of His Son, much more, being reconciled, we shall be saved by His life." (I prefer "in His life" instead of "by His life" as the translation of this last phrase.) As I noted previously, reconciliation or justification is by the blood, and salvation is by the resurrection. "And, having made peace [observe it is past tense, already accomplished] through the blood of His cross, by Him to reconcile all things unto Himself; by Him, I say, whether they be things in earth, or things in heaven" (Col. 1:20). Justification is peace, and peace is being reconciled to a relationship (see Rom. 5:1).

Please observe that the Colossians 1:20 says that God has reconciled all things to Himself in earth and in Heaven. He does not say, "in the underworld or under the earth." In Philippians 2:10, we find that Jesus Christ has been given a new name, at which every knee shall bow, "of those who are in heaven, and on earth, and under the earth" (NAS). Paul does not use this phrase "under the earth" in the Colossians passage because he is not addressing those who are condemned and residing in the underworld. When Jesus returns, on that day, the condemned spirit world will have no choice. They will bow and confess that Jesus Christ is Lord. It does not mean they will be saved by doing so. As the Book of Revelation testifies, all the rebellious society of mankind will bow before the believers and Christ and confess that God truly loved them. Still, God has not reconciled them to Himself. He has reconciled things in Heaven and things in earth, but not things in the "underworld."

The emphasis for things in Heaven and things in earth is reconciliation on God's part. God, by the cross, has reconciled Himself to the world. We become involved in that work when we believe the gospel.

> *And all things are of God, who hath reconciled us to Himself by Jesus Christ, and hath given to us the ministry of reconciliation* (2 Corinthians 5:18).

> *...God was in Christ reconciling the world to Himself, not counting their trespasses against*

them, and He has committed to us the word of reconciliation. Therefore, we are ambassadors for Christ, as though God were entreating through us; we beg you on behalf of Christ, be reconciled to God (2 Corinthians 5:19-20 NAS).

God is satisfying Himself first in the process of reconciliation.

We also should consider the word *satisfaction*, or *propitiation* as the Authorized Version uses it. Wherever you find that word in the New Testament, God is telling us that He has satisfied Himself for all the sin of all the world for all time. He had to do this before He could become reconciled to us. So what does it mean to us that God is reconciled to the world? It simply means that God is not angry anymore. God has reconciled Himself to all mankind, and He did so on the basis of the shed blood of propitiation.

Satisfaction, ransom, and redemption are all one-way streets. Reconciliation is a two-way street. Paul pleads, as an ambassador of Christ, "be ye reconciled to God." God is not angry with you anymore, and it is now time for you to stop being angry with Him. On what basis can you stop being angry with God? What made you angry with Him in the first place? The source is actually fear, which was the product of sin. Fear breeds hatred, and hatred breeds anger. What happened to the sin that bred the fear? It has been put away and the old man is crucified. "It is nailed to the cross and I bear it no more. Praise the Lord, praise the Lord, Oh, my soul" ("It Is Well With My Soul," H.G. Stafford). You do not have any reason to fear the wrath of God anymore.

Another profound result of this work of satisfaction is the basis of eternal judgment changes. Before, man was judged as a sinner and condemned like the first man, Adam. Now, Jesus Christ has paid for all sin, including the sin of Adam, which places the basis for judgment in the last Adam, Jesus Christ. In John 3:18 Jesus tells Nicodemus why the man who does not believe is condemned. Notice it is not because he is a sinner, but rather because he has not believed on the name of the only begotten Son of God. When the unregenerate come before the Great White Throne, the question placed before them will not be, "Are you a sinner?" but, "What have you done with Jesus who is called Christ?"

Because Jesus Christ has paid the full price for redemption, and because He has satisfied the Father for all sin in mankind, the Father has given His Son the right to judge the world. Jesus said, "For the Father judgeth no man, but hath committed all judgment unto the Son" (Jn. 5:22). The Holy Spirit was sent into the world to convict the world of sin, righteousness, and the judgment that is to come. The proclamation of this good news is called the "ministry of reconciliation."

Paul also mentions this in his first Epistle to Timothy. In it we read that Jesus "gave Himself a ransom for all, to be testified in due time" (1 Tim. 2:6). Later Paul says that the living God "is the Saviour of all men, specially of those that believe" (1 Tim. 4:10).

If God were to condemn men because they are sinners, then most surely we would all be lost because "there is none righteous" and "no man that sinneth not" (see Rom. 3:10; 1 Kings 8:46). The condemned man before God's throne in that day cannot plead ignorance or innocence, nor can he plead that he should be forgiven because other sinners worse than he were forgiven. Sinfulness, righteousness, sincerity, self-effort—none of these are even an issue. It is, "What have you done with Jesus who is called Christ?"

Atonement: Another important contrast between the Old and New Covenants is the use of the word *atonement.* Sin, under the Old Covenant, was not removed. There was no satisfaction for sin, rather, it was atoned for or covered over. In theological circles the term *atonement* is often used of the entire truth of Christ and His redemption. Technically, however, this usage is wrong, for it would apply only to redemption before the cross. Through Christ, God did not bring to pass "atonement." He brought to pass "satisfaction."

In Genesis 6:14, Noah is told to seal the ark by applying "pitch" or "tar." When you tar something, you cover it over to seal it. The Hebrew word used to describe this action is *kaphar* (pronounced ka-far). The Hebrew word *kipper* (pronounced key-pear) is based on the same root word and means "to atone." Atonement means simply "to cover" and when applied to sin, the sin is covered as if tar was applied. This word also appears in Leviticus 17:11: "For the life of the flesh is in the blood: and I have given it to you upon the altar to make an atonement for your souls...." The word *atonement* here is the Hebrew word *kipper*, meaning "to cover." The word is in use today by faithful Jews in the phrase *Yom Kippur*, which means "Day of Atonement."

Remission: In the Old Testament sins were covered by the atoning blood of bulls and goats. Sins were covered even though men of the Old Testament were justified by faith. Hebrews shows that it is impossible for the blood of bulls and goats to take away sins. Only through a better sacrifice could sin be wiped away. Under the New Covenant, God first of all satisfied Himself by the blood of Christ. He brought judgment on His Son and by Jesus' shed blood God's wrath on the world was erased. Through His blood, we now have "remission of sin." Remission means you are separated from your sin.

There are three references in particular that point out the transition from the old to the new economy:

For this is My blood of the new testament, which is shed for many for the remission of sins (Matthew 26:28).

And that repentance and remission of sins should be preached in His name among all nations... (Luke 24:47).

Now where remission of these is, there is no more offering for sin (Hebrews 10:18).

Each of these verses point out that sin is removed, or separated, from the believing sinner. Have you ever received a statement in the mail for a purchase and on the bottom, stamped in big red print, was, "PLEASE REMIT"? That means they want to separate you from your money. In our case, God has separated us from our debt and from our sin. There is no more "remembrance again made of sins" (see Heb. 10:2-3,18).

Sin: The word *sin* appears throughout the Bible in both the singular and the plural forms. Sin (singular) is the root or the nature of sin. Sins (plural) is the fruit or the activity of sin. It is very important to understand this distinction. Paul used the plural form in Galatians 1:4 to speak of the fruit—the activity of the root—which is the product of our actions. It is the root that is dealt with in the death of the old man. In his death, Christ shed His blood to deliver me from the root of sin. I died with Him and the statute of limitations for my sin ran out. You cannot charge or condemn one who is already condemned and executed. It is the fruit of sin that is now continually being dealt with by the blood of Jesus (see 1 Jn. 1:7–2:2). The death of Christ releases me from condemnation and the blood of Christ releases me from guilt.

When we were under sin, we were also under condemnation. Sins are the activities of the nature in the flesh which, in turn, results in guilt. How does God deal with the root of condemnation? Does He forgive? No, He does not. There is no forgiveness for condemnation, only death of the old man. "I have been crucified with Christ..." (Gal. 2:20 NAS). Because I died, I am free from condemnation and can be freed from guilt, which is the result of sins. "If we confess our sins, He is faithful and righteous to forgive us our sins and to cleanse us from all unrighteousness" (1 Jn. 1:9 NAS).

Guilt: The dietary laws were given in the Old Testament because guilt had not been removed yet. The law was given so the whole world would become guilty before God (see Rom. 3:19). When guilt functions in the personality, the body cannot throw off or assimilate substances it could otherwise handle. More and more evidence is coming from the medical community that indicate our immune systems can be interrupted by various kinds of stress—one of the most prevalent being guilt. Guilt hinders the proper functions of the body. Now that we can, through His righteousness, walk in forgiveness and peace of heart, we can, in effect, drink any deadly thing and it will not hurt us (see Mk. 16:18). Most believers have not come to walk in this degree of rest.

Another illustration is the law that deals with jealousy, found in Numbers 5. If a spirit of jealousy came over a man and he believed his wife had been unfaithful, she was to be brought before the priest. Taken into the sanctuary, a bitter concoction was made of water and the dust of the floor of the tabernacle. She then had to drink that concoction. If she was guilty, her thigh would rot and she would die. If she were not guilty, she would not be harmed. Here we can see the effect of guilt and the effect of peace. This Old Testament story shows us how great and glorious our position is since our High Priest, Jesus, by and through Himself, took the urn of bitter water from our hands and drank on our behalf. He took our guilt that we might go free and unharmed.

A profound illustration of Christ bearing our guilt is found in the analogy of the serpent on the pole. Jesus said, "And as Moses lifted up the serpent in the wilderness, even so must the Son of man be lifted up" (Jn. 3:14). The event in the wilderness (see Num. 21:6-9) becomes a picture of His own work on the cross. The words of Jesus in the garden are most remarkable: "My Father, if it is possible, let this cup pass from Me" (Mt. 26:39 NAS). I used to think He was anticipating the cross, but it was much more than that. Throughout His entire ministry He knew the cross was waiting for Him. So what was unique about this "cup"? When Jesus looked into the cup, He saw for the first time something that caused Him to draw back in anguish. He saw the full import of what lay before Him. In taking our place in communion with "that old serpent, called the Devil, and Satan" (Rev. 12:9), He would become the serpent on the pole.

Picture the day of the crucifixion. From the third hour to the ninth hour there was the light of the sun. God had been in fellowship with His Son and the blood of the Lamb was being shed. He was the Lamb of God taking away the sin of the world, a Lamb without spot or blemish. God could fellowship with that Lamb and look on with approval. In fact, He was doing just that, approving of the Lamb that was satisfying Him for the sin of the world. Then the darkness came, and Jesus cried out, "My God, My God, why hast Thou forsaken Me?" (Mt. 27:46) That is when the Lamb became the serpent and the heavens went dark. Never before had fellowship been broken in the Godhead. Then the judgment of God fell and He, who knew no sin, was made sin for us (see 2 Cor. 5:21).

At that moment, Jesus drank that awful communion cup in our stead. In First Corinthians 10:16 we read, "The cup of blessing which we bless, is it not the communion of the blood of Christ? The bread which we break, is it not the communion of the body of Christ?" The word *communion* means fellowship, or "common union." What Jesus received in that cup was a communion with our sin and satan in order that He might deliver us from the bondage into which satan had brought us. He became, before the Father, the total expression of all that was evil. That is what is so profound and is the experience from which He shrank. It is too overwhelming to consider, but the fact is, that was the only way He could ever set us free from the bondage of sin.

Remember, before anyone can become an intercessor he must enter into the place of the one for whom he is interceding. Jesus entered into that place where I was bound in fellowship with satan in a common union. But it was impossible that death should hold Jesus (see Acts 2:24). Death was holding me, but it could not hold Him. He came into that place to get me out, to set me free. He came without fear, knowing He would return, knowing He would succeed. His confidence did not make any less serious the bitter water He had to swallow. He drank that we might be set free to be with Him in freedom forever. As the Lamb, He gave me righteousness, but as the serpent, He gave me salvation.

Grace Reigns: When we came into the world through the first Adam, we came in sin. We were under condemnation, and condemnation requires death as its penalty.

> *Therefore, just as through one man sin entered into the world, and death through sin, and so death spread to all men, because all sinned— ... For if by the transgression of the one, death reigned through the one, much more those who receive the abundance of grace and of the gift of righteousness will reign in life through the One, Jesus Christ* (Romans 5:12,17 NAS).

We also were placed under servitude to sin. Because of our sin nature, we came under the dominion or reign of sin. That produced sin and guilt. This is what Paul says in Romans 5:17. For this we have forgiveness and cleansing by His blood. But how did He deal with the reign of sin?

Romans 5:12 told us how we got into this death and slavery. That is, "death reigned through one" (Rom 5:17). Now the reign of the old man, or the reign of sin, must be broken before we can walk in the salvation of God. That is the difference between ransom and redemption. The price is paid, which satisfies the ransom. Now redemption is necessary. We need to be retrieved from death. How is that accomplished? Death is twofold, just as birth is twofold. I was born first in sin and now, I am born again in righteousness. We died in sin in the first Adam, but we must now die to sin in the last Adam. Remember Paul's words: "...we thus judge, that if one died for all, then were all dead" (2 Cor. 5:14). The death of the old man breaks the reign of sin and brings me under the reign of grace. It also brings me under the authority and nature of the last Adam.

"So then as through one transgression there resulted condemnation to all men, even so through one act of righteousness there resulted justification of life to all men" (Rom. 5:18 NAS). Just as we came into the world under the first Adam and into his death, under the last Adam we come into His righteousness, life, and peace. We enter peace with God, peace from God, and the peace of God, which are progressions in our growth.

For as through the one man's disobedience the many were made sinners, even so through the obedience of the One the many will be made righteous. And the Law came in that the transgression might increase; but where sin increased, grace abounded all the more, that, as sin reigned in death, even so grace might reign through righteousness to eternal life through Jesus Christ our Lord (Romans 5:19-21 NAS).

God has established His righteousness and grace reigns. Grace reigns! We have been loosed from the condemnation of death and brought into life by the resurrection of Jesus Christ. We experience this life when the Holy Spirit enters into our spirit and makes us a fit temple for God's Spirit. Since we have been reconciled to Him, grace reigns instead of sin. It is an important distinction because we do what we know and we reckon on what we understand.

In verse 21 you see the phrase "as sin reigned." In offsetting sin's reign, God did not say righteousness reigned; rather He said grace reigns. Because God is righteous and His righteousness has been established in us, so now grace reigns. If you fall flat on your face, grace is still reigning. You did not put grace on the throne and you cannot bring grace down from the throne. God put grace on the throne; thus grace reigns overall who believe. So even though we fall, we shall not be utterly cast down. In every place and at all time the Lord upholds us with His hand (see Ps. 37:24) because grace reigns.

"Even so consider yourselves to be dead to sin, but alive to God in Christ Jesus" (Rom. 6:11 NAS). As we observed in Chapter 4, the word *consider* is the same word translated "impute." It simply means to "count so." You "count so" what God says is so. Whether you count it so or not, the truth of God's Word will not change. You will simply enjoy His benefits a great deal more if you agree with God. No doubt you have heard the expression "God said it, I believe it, and that settles it." That is not correct. God said it and that settles it whether I believe it or not. It is forever settled in Heaven (see Ps. 119:89). God says we are to reckon on what He has done, know that our old man is crucified, and know that Christ was raised from the dead and dies no more. Because of all this, we can reckon ourselves to be dead unto sin indeed and alive to God. We reckon on what is so and then go and be what we are.

"Therefore do not let sin reign in your mortal body, that you should obey its lusts" (Rom. 6:12 NAS). How does sin reign? Sin reigns through the law and through the condemnation of the law, which sin brings. Paul is not referring here to what we do, as he is to how we react to what we do. We are brought into bondage by the condemnation of sin. If we remain under condemnation, then peace is gone and guilt comes. When guilt comes, so do all manner of problems. "For sin shall not be master over you..." (Rom. 6:14a NAS). Sin is not reigning over us, so it cannot have dominion over us. Sin has been de-throned. Why? "For you are not under the law, but under grace" (Rom 6:14b NAS).

Notice Paul did not say that sin will not be master over you because you won't sin anymore. Rather, he said that sin will not be master over you because law is no longer the criteria used to judge you. Grace is the criteria that judges you. Grace, then, is an imputation to you of what you do not have. Mercy is God not giving you what you deserve, but giving you what you do not deserve. God's grace provides you with all that you are not and your faith is imputed for righteousness (see Rom. 4:3).

Body of Sin: At the root of all sanctification is separation from the body of sin. "Knowing this, that our old self was crucified with Him, that our body of sin might be done away with, that we should no longer be slaves to sin" (Rom. 6:6 NAS). The reality of this separation from the body of sin causes Paul to say, "But if I am doing the very thing I do not wish, I am no longer the one doing it, but sin which dwells in me" (Rom. 7:20 NAS). Amazing! Paul said, "I did not do it. Sin that dwells in me did it."

You might say, "What a cop-out!" It is not a cop-out. In truth it is a grand act of grace on the part of a redeeming God. Your life is hidden with Christ in God (see Col. 3:3), and the old guilty man has died on the cross. That dead old man cannot be charged with guilt and the new man is not guilty. Thus God, because of the finished work of the cross, refuses to impute sin to the new man (see 2 Cor. 5:19).

It staggers me when I think that God sees me separated from the body of sin. In fact, I am so separated that Paul says if I sin, it is not me who does it, but the sin that dwells in me. I did not do it. Sin that dwells in me did it. I may be grieved over it, but the blood is still available to keep guilt from overcoming me. I need to be sensitive so I can quickly confess. This keeps me walking in the light, but with it, I must also remember that the Father sees sin separate and apart from me in Christ. The cross has "drawn a line" between the person I am in Christ and the person I was in Adam. Therefore, Paul says the body of sin is dead, but the Spirit is life because of His righteous act at the cross.

Paul shows us in Romans 6:12-13 that the body is where sin resides. It works in our members, or our appetites, which work through this "earthly house." Throughout Romans 6 and 7, Paul warns of the body's propensity to sin and our spirit's desire for righteousness. In Romans 7:24, we can feel his anguish as he sees himself as a wretched man because of the body of death that would drive him to sin.

In declaring the road to deliverance through Jesus Christ, Paul summarizes both chapters with one phrase: "...So then with the mind I myself serve the law of God; but with the flesh the law of sin" (Rom. 7:25). As long as we are in this body, those drives will persist. What is Paul's answer? He devotes Romans 8, to telling us we will receive a new body that will no longer have an appetite for sin.

Chapter 8 in Romans has three dominant messages. First, the believer is in the sphere of the Spirit and no longer in the sphere of the flesh or under condemnation. Second, there is a "groaning" in the believer because of his body, which anticipates its re-demption. (Remember, the spirit of man is re-deemed; the soul is being redeemed; the body will be redeemed). Third, the believer is about to receive a new body and with patience waits for it. This new body will be the final blow to the operation of sin in the saint.

> *So when this corruptible shall have put on in-corruption, and this mortal shall have put on immortality, then shall be brought to pass the saying that is written, Death is swallowed up in victory. O death, where is thy sting? O grave, where is thy victory? The sting of death is sin; and the strength of sin is the law. But thanks be to God, which giveth us the victory through our Lord Jesus Christ* (1 Corinthians 15:54-57).

Since it was not possible for death to hold Jesus in the grave, neither will it be possible for death to hold the saints in the grave. (Those who are alive at His return will not be held by the world.) We will receive a new body like His glorious body and we will, in that day, be conformed to the image of the Son.

As long as we are in this body, we will continue to "miss the mark." Paul says, "For all have sinned [completed action in past time], and come short [pres-ent tense] of the glory of God" (Rom. 3:23). As long as we are without our "house which is from heaven," we must face this one in the present. To walk in peace, while in this body, we must know that we have died to the law. The "statute of limitations" has run out on the believer and he cannot be brought into "double jeopardy." He has been tried, convicted, and executed. We have died to the law, and the law has died to us.

For I through the law am dead to the law, that I might live unto God. ... Christ hath redeemed us from the curse of the law, being made a curse for us: for it is written, Cursed is every one that hangeth on a tree (Galatians 2:19, 3:13).

Jesus Christ has removed the law that condemns us and we cannot be condemned or hung, for there is nothing written against us. "For where no law is, there is no transgression" (Rom. 4:15b).

The law is not a problem to someone who is not a lawbreaker. Adam, in the Garden, was under the law. He could eat of any of the fruit of the trees except the tree of the knowledge of good and evil. He was under the law, but Adam was not a lawbreaker. That tree did not bother Adam at all. It was not until the woman he loved became a tool of the serpent that he became a lawbreaker. Paul said, "But we know that the law is good, if a man use it lawfully; knowing this, that the law is not made for a righteous man, but for the lawless..." (1 Tim. 1:8-9).

In our new position, God does not reckon us to be lawbreakers anymore. "But I do fail," you say. Of course you do, but the point is, God does not impute that to you. Remember, "...God was in Christ reconciling the world to Himself, not counting their trespasses against them..." (2 Cor. 5:19 NAS). That is how we are able to recover and that is why we can walk in peace.

This does not release someone to walk in sin; rather it releases them to walk in righteousness. They are released to walk in joy. They are released to walk in peace. "The sting of death is sin, and the power of sin is the law; but thanks be to God, who gives us the victory through our Lord Jesus Christ" (1 Cor. 15:56-57 NAS). It is not through our own righteousness, but through the righteousness of Jesus. It is because of this truth that Paul is free to admonish us: "Therefore, my beloved brethren, be ye stedfast, unmoveable, always abounding in the work of the Lord, forasmuch as ye know that your labour is not in vain in the Lord" (1 Cor. 15:58).

Paul is simply teaching us that we are established in righteousness. We cannot impose any other law, system, or rules to increase our position before God. We are already perfect in God's sight. We are perfect in our relationship before God, for it is established in Christ. We can walk in peace with the Spirit of His Son in our heart, crying, "Abba, Father." Therefore, He can bring us into a walk in sonship, which is a personal and intimate relationship with Himself. The Epistle to the Galatians addresses the believer's position in sonship. "...God has sent forth the Spirit of His Son into our hearts, crying, 'Abba! Father!' " (Gal. 4:6 NAS) The word *abba*, or *AbbA*, is an Aramaic form of the Hebrew word, *Ab*, and it comes into our vernacular as "daddy." Out of that relationship will come the practical righteousness of

God, which is the solution to sin. In view of this new position we are called to a new relationship. "Be ye holy, for I the Lord your God am holy" (see 1 Pet. 1:16). God is separate from the society of this world, and He is calling on His people to be separate unto Himself. Second Corinthians 6:17-18 reads, " 'Therefore, come out from their midst and be separate,' says the Lord. 'And do not touch what is unclean; and I will welcome you. And I will be a father to you, and you shall be sons and daughters to Me,' says the Lord Almighty" (NAS).

Chapter 6

Paul's Gospel

How deep was Paul's concern for the churches he was a father and an apostle over? Any doctrine that threatened their liberty in Christ was met with firm resistance. The men who created the furor were not just concerned with ceremonial rituals; they were attempting to impose moral law and the ceremonial laws that went along with it. This passage in Romans illustrate this:

> *I say then, Hath God cast away His people? God forbid. For I also am an Israelite, of the seed of Abraham, of the tribe of Benjamin. God hath not cast away His people which He foreknew. Wot ye not what the scripture saith of Elias* [Elijah]? *how he maketh intercession to God against Israel, saying, Lord, they have killed Thy prophets, and digged down Thine altars; and I am left alone, and they seek my life. But what saith the answer of God unto him? I have reserved to Myself seven thousand*

men, who have not bowed the knee to the image of Baal. Even so then at this present time also there is a remnant according to the election of grace (Romans 11:1-5).

Take note of verse 6: "And if by grace, then is it no more of works: otherwise grace is no more grace. But if it be of works, then is it no more grace: otherwise work is no more work."

Throughout this part of his epistle, Paul deals with the nation of Israel and her response to God through the ages. As he deals with Israel, he also provides us with a grand lesson about law and grace, or perhaps I should say, work and grace. Verse 6 is the capstone of Paul's message. We cannot and we must not mix works and grace, law and faith, flesh and Spirit. Paul is consistent throughout his epistles in maintaining a separation of these issues.

Paul tells us that the Old Testament and the law is for our "admonition and learning." There is a lesson for us from Deuteronomy 22:9,11.

Thou shalt not sow thy vineyard with divers seeds: lest the fruit of thy seed which thou hast sown, and the fruit of thy vineyard, be defiled. ... Thou shalt not wear a garment of divers sorts, as of woollen and linen together.

The word "seed" is used as a metaphor for the Word of God and garments are a metaphor for the covering that God uses to cover our unrighteousness. The point is, "divers seeds" will grow and contaminate the seed you wanted to remain pure. Paul said that the law is holy, just, and spiritual, but it must not be "sown" with the New Covenant message of grace. With garments, each type of material has a purpose and a time—linen in summer, wool in winter. If you wear wool in the summer you will sweat, which reminds us of the sweat under the curse of self-effort. Romans 9:16 summarizes this for us: "So then it does not depend on the man who wills or the man who runs, but on God who has mercy" (NAS).

We can learn two things from Paul in this passage: the basis upon which the sinner comes to Christ and the criteria by which the believer is judged in Christ. The sinner comes to Christ by the grace of God, through faith. He is judged by grace through the faithfulness of Jesus Christ. We have stated before that we had obtained death through the first man, Adam; we have obtained life through the last Adam, Jesus Christ. In the first Adam, we did good things and bad things. The good things could not make us better, and the bad things could not make us worse.

Jesus, in the course of His ministry, raised three people from the dead. One was a young girl, who had just died and whose body had not yet begun to decay. The second was a young man who was on the way to his grave and whose body was beginning to decay. The third was a man who had been in the grave four days and whose body stunk with decay. Now, all three of these were in different degrees of death. So it was with the believer before his new birth. He is dead in sin, but some manifest the effect of death more than others.

We are in the life and righteousness of Jesus Christ—and that is an absolute. In and by the new birth we have died to death and are made alive in His life. The new birth was necessary to deliver us from the old man and the former relationship in Adam. Believing the record that God gave concerning His Son is sufficient to bring the convicted sinner into Christ. It is not by works of righteousness; we are justified by faith. This is the message of Paul and it is the essence of Romans 5:12-21. The unregenerate are who they are because of one man. The regenerate (born again) are who they are because of one Man, Jesus, the Christ and Federal Head of a new race of redeemed people.

Motives

Why do I serve Him? Is it because He is pleased with me? Do I serve Him in order to please Him? On the contrary, my relationship with the Father is established and maintained by the grace of God. Some believers ask, "Do you believe in salvation by grace?" "Yes, I believe in salvation by grace." Then they ask, "What part does works play in salvation?" Paul's epistles to the Romans and the Galatians confirm God's salvation is not dependent on works.

But to him that worketh not, but believeth on Him that justifieth the ungodly, his faith is counted for righteousness. Even as David also describeth the blessedness of the man, unto whom God imputeth righteousness without works, saying, Blessed are they whose iniquities are forgiven, and whose sins are covered (Romans 4:5-7).

In Romans 3:21, Paul said that the righteousness of God was witnessed by the law and the prophets. Romans 4 cites two witnesses, Abraham and David, and both testify to the reckoning of righteousness apart from works. Both of these men failed God and were willfully disobedient, but both saw their failure replaced with God's success.

Kinds of Works

In the epistles, "works" are referred to in a number of different ways. First, there are "good works." Paul exhorted Titus to encourage the saints to "...maintain good works. These things are good and profitable unto men" (Tit. 3:8). This kind of work is born out of the constraining love of God. They are not requirements, but are voluntary acts to give help where needed. This is the kind of work that lays up treasure in Heaven.

Second, there are "dead works." The writer of Hebrews tells us of a conscience "purged from dead works to serve the living God" (see Heb. 9:14). Dead works are good things done for the wrong reason. They may serve some worldly cause, but have no eternal value ("Let the dead bury their dead" [Lk. 9:60]). Although all of these qualify as works, the most grievous to the Lord is work done to obtain or to maintain our relationship or right standing with

Him. Paul called the Galatians foolish because they were trying to achieve maturity by fleshly efforts.

Then there is the "work of faith." This work is a threefold grace in which the believer is occupied. "Remembering without ceasing your work of faith, and labour of love, and patience of hope in our Lord Jesus Christ, in the sight of God and our Father" (1 Thess. 1:3). The work of faith is the product of believing the Word of the Lord. Paul said, "Through [Him] we have received grace and apostleship to bring about the obedience of faith among all the Gentiles, for His name's sake" (Rom. 1:5 NAS). True faith believes God and, therefore, will obey God. A work that is born of faith will be a fruitful one. When the seed of faith is sown, it produces a crop, either large or small, but always with His approval. Paul illustrates this same principle in First Corinthians 3:10-15. The warning is to take heed in choosing the material with which we build the house. It may be built of wood, hay, or stubble; it may be built of gold, silver, or precious stones. It is not the appearance of the house that is called into question, but the material out of which it is built. "...I laid a foundation, and another is building upon it. But let each man be careful how he builds upon it" (1 Cor. 3:10 NAS). The material refers to the content of our message and our motive for building. In Paul's situation, he was dealing with a legalistic message and the motive was to avoid the persecution that comes with preaching the pure grace of God. That is what he refers to when he says, "...lest they should suffer persecution for the cross of Christ...that they may glory in your flesh" (Gal. 6:12-13). Too many ministries have the appearance of godliness and usefulness, but are in fact only monuments to powerful personalities and their natural talents. They offer a "show time" mentality and, even worse, an appetite for money. This runs against the character of the New Testament and may well be judged as wood, hay, and stubble when Jesus returns. Jesus said, "For that which is highly esteemed among men is abomination in the sight of God" (Lk. 16:15b). What we believe to be lively and exciting may, in God's sight, be a dead work.

Another Gospel

Paul's concern for the Galatians is evident in the first few verses of his epistle to them. "I am amazed that you are so quickly deserting Him who called you by the grace of Christ, for a different gospel" (Gal. 1:6 NAS). This gospel was not good news, but law wrapped in religion.

> But even though we, or an angel from heaven, should preach to you a gospel contrary to that which we have preached to you, let him be accursed. As we have said before, so I say again now, if any man is preaching to you a gospel contrary to that which you received, let him be accursed (Galatians 1:8-9 NAS).

The term *accursed* or *anathema* describes a condition that produces serious consequences. This cursed "gospel" that the legalizers were bringing was a message of "right action." These messengers were disguised as ministers of righteousness (see 2 Cor. 11:13-15).

They were preaching the "tree of the knowledge of good and evil." They were saying that to do right is to be like God. No believer in Christ would be deceived by a message that told him to do evil, but to require righteous action seems plausible. If someone says to us, "You must love God," we agree immediately that we should, so we make a sincere effort to do so. The sad result is we may offer a love that is not sincere. We learn quickly that it is only by the Spirit pouring His love into our hearts that we can love Him. It is the "truth" that sets us free. It is not what is true, but rather the "truth." It is true that we should love God. It is also true that we do not. The "truth" is that God loves us anyhow. That is the gospel, and that is good news. That is the message of the "tree of life." Does this seem to be missing from much of our preaching today?

Those who put emphasis on works to obtain or maintain right standing with God are always legalistic or doctrinal in their approach to the message of the gospel. "God has done His part, so we must do our part," they say. They believe that once God has accomplished His work, we must maintain our relationship by how we behave. What makes this subtle approach appealing is that it sounds right.

Many years ago I was talking to a Mormon about redemption. His comment was, "It is like buying a house. Jesus made the down payment, and now we must keep up the payments." I told him that I was a bankrupt sinner and had no way of keeping up the payments. Some would say, "Well, that is a cult. What would you expect?" Sadly, I must say there is little difference in that Mormon's statement and many of the messages we hear today.

In accepting a doctrine of works as valid we become victims to one or both of the following: If we are reasonably successful, we become self-righteous; if we fail, which is more probable, we are condemned. We condemn ourselves because we feel that we failed God. We also are condemned by those who put us under this bondage because we failed to make them look good. Paul said that the legalizers like to "glory in your flesh."

Incidentally, when I speak of legalism, I am not talking about the law of Moses only. Legalism is any set of rules that purport to bring us to maturity or into right standing with God. Paul said, "...If there had been a law given which could have given life, verily righteousness should have been by [or out of] the law" (Gal. 3:21). Again, it is not just by *the* law, but by *any* law.

The gift and office of the prophet is primarily concerned with righteousness. The prophet is always setting the plumb line for a walk in righteousness. Often the prophet is not very popular. The process of building construction is a good example of prophecy in righteousness (see Eph. 4:11-12). The apostle establishes the foundation, and the evangelist brings the material for the construction. Teachers instruct the laborers and the pastor runs the infirmary. The prophet is the building inspector, and he is constantly checking to see if the building is being constructed properly.

We often do not like the fellow who comes in with the plumb line. He holds the line up to the wall to see if it is straight. He says, "This is not plumb. You must fix it." Or perhaps he says, "That window is higher than the architect's plans require. You must lower it." It is comparable to going into a lady's house with a pair of white gloves and wiping the tops of all the doorjambs. You can imagine how much she would appreciate your inspection.

In this phase of growth, the priest speaks to God for man, but the prophet speaks to man for God. The righteousness that the prophet preaches has, as its goal, the spiritual health and safety of the believer. For example, the apostle Paul does not confront the Corinthian believers concerning an incestuous relationship among their membership, saying, "Do you not know the seventh commandment says, 'thou shalt not commit adultery'?" Instead, he says, "...shall I then take the members of Christ, and make them the members of a harlot? God forbid" (1 Cor. 6:15). He did not put them under the law or impose the penalty of the law. Instead, he appealed to their relationship in the Body of Christ. What a magnificent difference! In the one case we appeal to a commandment that causes death. In the other case we appeal to a relationship of love that brings life. "The letter killeth, but the spirit giveth life" (2 Cor. 3:6).

Love Relationship

The "other gospel" preaches a merit-based relationship that cannot edify. The epistle to the Hebrews tells us the law could do nothing to bring maturity; rather, it slays us for not being able to meet the standard others have set. This tends to divert our attention from the indwelling Christ to a well-meaning but unable self.

> *Would to God ye could bear with me a little in my folly: and indeed bear with me. For I am jealous over you with godly jealousy: for I have espoused you to one husband, that I may present you as a chaste virgin to Christ* (2 Corinthians 11:1-2).

Throughout the New Testament, the relationship between Christ and the Church is seen as a relationship between a bridegroom and his bride. Is it necessary for a husband to put any sort of legal injunction on his wife to make sure she fulfills her responsibilities? It goes without saying that such a thing would strain any marriage to the breaking point.

I love my wife very much and we have had a wonderful marriage for nearly three decades. We have no rules for each other, but like all couples, we do have preferences. If I wish for her to be more attentive in some area, I don't demand it of her. I must "love her into doing it." She knows exactly what I am trying to do to her, but she responds anyway and does so willingly. God made woman to be a receiver and man to be a giver.

Nowhere in the New Testament is a wife ever told to love her husband. In Titus 2:4 women are exhorted to "love their husbands," but the word translated love is not *agape*, it is *phileo*. They are to have an affection for their husbands. On the other hand, the husband is told to love (*agape*) his wife "as Christ also loved the church, and gave Himself for it" (Eph. 5:25).

Paul said this husband/wife relationship is a picture of Christ and the Church (see Eph. 5:32). From this picture we can see some important parallels. Nowhere under the New Covenant is the believer ever told to love God. Again, our minds go to the Gospels where more than once we are reminded of the first commandment. It must be remembered that the Gospels are not the New Covenant. That does not begin until the veil of the temple is rent in two and we enter the Most Holy Place by the blood of Jesus. "This cup is the new testament in My blood, which is shed for you," Jesus said (Lk. 22:20). It was at the cross that the New Covenant began. From there on we are never told to love God. Certainly we should, but telling us to do so would do no better than it did under the law. What does the New Covenant say? "Herein is love, not that we loved God, but that He loved us, and sent His Son to be the propitiation for our sins" (1 Jn. 4:10). "...The love of God is shed abroad in our hearts by the Holy Ghost which is given unto us" (Rom. 5:5). Love begets love and if a man wants his wife to love him, then he must first love her. Christ wanted us to love Him, so He first loved us.

"The fear of the Lord is clean," the psalmist said (see Ps. 19:9). There are no impurities in Him. We need not be concerned that God is planning some sort of trap for us to fall into, however. He is not devious, nor is He underhanded in His affairs. Therefore, we need not be afraid of the "fear of the Lord." There is no shadow of turning in Him (see Jas. 1:17). What He was yesterday, He will be tomorrow. We are not consumed because He is what He says He is. He is not moody and He is not prone to sudden fits of change that will threaten His attitude toward His people. The God and Father of our Lord Jesus Christ is a loving and compassionate Savior.

This is the same Savior who said, "...Yea, I have loved thee with an everlasting love: therefore with lovingkindness have I drawn thee" (Jer. 31:3). This is the same Savior who said, "All that the Father giveth Me shall come to Me; and him that cometh to Me I will in no wise cast out" (Jn. 6:37). This is the same Savior who said, "Father, I will that they also, whom Thou hast given Me, be with Me where I am; that they may behold My glory, which Thou hast given Me: for Thou lovedst Me before the foundation of the world" (Jn. 17:24).

Scripture is full of verses just like these. The point is, He is the author and finisher of the believer's redemption. Why is it so difficult for believers to walk in His love? The only rule He would have us walk by is just that—His love. He said, "Henceforth I call you not servants; for the servant knoweth not what his lord doeth: but I have called you friends; for all things that I have heard of My Father I have made known unto you" (Jn. 15:15). Abraham was the friend of God and Abraham needed no rules to govern his walk. He trusted God, and God trusted him. Yes, Abraham did fail. Is it not encouraging for the Spirit to record those shortcomings in His friend? Can we not trust such a God and such a Friend? The manner with which God governs His people is through His faithful love.

The Chastening of the Lord

Maturity in Christ is God's priority for us. According to the apostle Peter, He has given us all things that are necessary to life and godliness (see 2 Pet. 1:13). Now He wants to work in us by His Spirit to help us achieve a faithful walk. Faithfulness is always the key. It is not a matter of how successful we are, but how faithful we are. "Moreover it is required in stewards, that a man be found faithful" (1 Cor. 4:2). We will be judged by our consistent pursuit of His ways.

John speaks to this issue in his first epistle. He says, "And now, little children, abide in Him, so that when He appears, we may have confidence and not shrink away from Him in shame at His coming" (1 Jn. 2:28 NAS). What a disappointment it would be to come before Him in that day only to learn, for the first time, how greatly He loved us. We would have nothing but shame for how we responded to that love.

To maintain the safety and to encourage the maturity of the one who is loved, love must do all that is required of it. Hebrews tells us that God chastens all of His children. Without that discipline any claim to sonship would be an illegitimate claim. Chastening can run the range from a simple rebuke like, "The Cretians are always liars...Wherefore rebuke them sharply" (Tit. 1:12-13), to a serious judgment like, "deliver such an one unto Satan for the destruction of the flesh, that the spirit may be saved in the day of the Lord Jesus" (1 Cor. 5:5). We must not mistake His discipline for a lack of love on His part. In truth, it is evidence of His love.

The way we respond to His love is based on our knowledge of His affection for us. The more we understand His love, the more sincere our response to Him will be. "But I fear, lest by any means, as the serpent beguiled Eve through his subtilty, so your minds should be corrupted from the simplicity that is in Christ" (2 Cor. 11:3). The problem is Christ's way is too simple for some.

For if he that cometh preacheth another Jesus [another of the same kind] *whom we have not preached, or if ye receive another spirit* [another of a different kind] *which ye have not received, or another gospel* [of a different kind] *which ye have not accepted, ye might well bear with him* (2 Corinthians 11:4).

Paul was using a bit of sarcasm here. Men had come preaching the same kind of Jesus, but a different kind of spirit and a different kind of gospel. The error was revealed when it did not work. It brought death to the people of God. It contradicts the words that the risen Son of God spoke to Paul when Paul was caught up to the third heaven.

Paul goes on in chapter 11 to say this:

For such men are false apostles, deceitful workers, disguising themselves as apostles of Christ. And no wonder, for even Satan disguises himself as an angel of light [not of darkness]. *Therefore it is not surprising if his servants also disguise themselves as servants of righteousness; whose end shall be according to their deeds* (2 Corinthians 11:13-15 NAS).

This is a remarkable statement. When they come to put us under a legalistic ritual, they come preaching righteousness. That is what makes it sound so plausible. They convince us by appealing to what we already know—God desires righteousness. The problem is, if the burden of righteousness—and performing righteously and maintaining a righteous position—is placed on me, I am no better off now than when I was under the demands of the law. That is what makes it an *heteros* gospel, a different kind of gospel.

The gospel Paul preached declared that the righteousness of God in Christ has been imputed to me totally apart from anything I am, ever had, or ever hope to be. Through Christ, I am firmly established in a position of righteousness. If my obedience to Him is not out of my knowledge of His great love for me, then it will all be an outward show. I may look good, I may make my church look good, but my heart will be far from Him.

We are to grow in grace and in knowledge of the Lord and Savior, Jesus Christ. If I am willing to grow in grace, then I can grow in knowledge. If I am not willing to grow in grace, then I will never grow in knowledge. Grace reminds me of my own inadequacies. If I am inclined to take credit for any success, then further revelations of Him will not be forthcoming. If, however, I know it is Him and not my own ability, then I am entrusted with His truth.

The perfect vessel for satan's use is not the "drunk in the gutter." Given a choice, satan would choose the preacher who spouts rules, regulations, and laws from the pulpit. Sinful people are going to do sinful things without a lot of satan's help. But if he is to snare the committed Christian, he must do it in an area that is of deep concern to the Christian. That area is his desire to please God. Satan, then, puts up a religious smoke screen: "Just be religious and do righteously, and God has to approve of you." God does not "have to" do anything except agree with His Son. So if we are not in the Son, all is lost. The problem with our righteousness is that it is ours.

Jesus dealt much more severely with people who were righteous outwardly than He did with blatant sinners. He said He had "not come to call the righteous, but sinners to repentance" (Mt. 9:13). The self-righteous have no idea that they need to repent and resent being told they do. "It is not the man that is whole that needs a physician," Jesus said, "but the one that is sick" (see Mt. 9:12). That is the reason I say, "Good people can go to hell, and bad people can go to Heaven." Since good people do not think they need to repent, they go to hell because of their self-righteousness. Our sin is no problem for God. We know that is an abomination to God. Our real problem is our righteousness. Remember the words of Isaiah, "But we are all as an unclean thing, and all our righteousnesses are as filthy rags" (Is. 64:6a). Did you notice that the word *righteousness* is in the plural? That means all of our "acts of righteousness." If we do not stand in Him, we do not stand at all.

A Curse in an Age of Blessing

There is a curse pronounced on anyone who would come preaching any gospel other than the one Paul preached (see Gal.1:8-9). Curses are not common in the New Testament. Therefore, such preaching must be a serious matter for such strong language to be used. The message of God is at risk here.

Proverbs tells us that "the curse that is without a cause will not come" (see Prov. 26:2b). What is the cause that would bring such an anathema on someone who teaches the Scripture? After all, Paul said to the Philippians that some were preaching Christ for all the wrong reasons, but he still rejoiced because Christ was being preached (see Phil. 1:16-18). Even an insincere heart did not bring down a curse. There must have been something especially important about Paul's message. What is so unique about it? His message offered us redemption apart from our works, salvation without our contribution, and the assurance of heaven by faith alone. That seems so elementary, yet when one considers the emphasis that is so often placed on our responsibility, the warning to those who would destroy Paul's message becomes important.

The Lord wants us to walk with Him in purity and holiness. But the heart of Paul's gospel is that regardless of how well we walk with Him, we are still His. Such an idea raised the ire of the legalists of Paul's day and raises the self-righteous hackles of the legalists of our day. Remember, a legalist required a standard of performance for a believer to maintain his right standing with God. This was the reason for the curse. A curse was brought on the earth because man ate of the "tree of the knowledge of good and evil." The emphasis of the gospel of Jesus Christ is not a knowledge of good things and bad things. The gospel is the "tree of life." Life dispels all death. Life brings forth fruit naturally without a struggle. It is His life in us that makes laws unnecessary. "For the law made nothing perfect..." (Heb. 7:19). All law can do is condemn the believer for his failure. If the message of the legalist keeps the believer from growing to maturity in Christ, and if it can only condemn the believer for his failure, is it any wonder that those who preach such a message would be under a curse?

Jesus said, "It is the spirit that quickeneth; the flesh profiteth nothing: the words that I speak unto you, they are spirit, and they are life" (Jn. 6:63). The Tree of Life, which is Jesus Christ, is the only source of a righteous life that honors God and not self. "...If ye continue in My word, then are ye My disciples indeed; and ye shall know the truth, and the truth shall make you free" (Jn. 8:31-32). The Word of God is the seed of God's life. To "ingest" His Word is to ingest His life. As it grows in the believer, it will displace all that is not of Him.

"I will never forget Thy precepts: for with them Thou hast quickened me" (Ps. 119:93). This establishes a new value system in the believer. He presents his body for God to live in and, as a result, his mind is renewed. The things that were once natural are now unnatural and the things that were unnatural are now natural. Instead of a propensity to sin, he now has a propensity to righteousness.

The duty of the believer is to hunger after the Lord. The psalmist said, "And I will walk at liberty: for I seek Thy precepts" (Ps. 119:45). To hunger after the Lord and become conscious of His love brings a spontaneous response in me. It is a natural growth that God, by His Word, brings about in the believer. Now I can walk at perfect liberty. I walk in perfect liberty because there is a new kind of inner restraint upon me. "For what the Law could not do, weak as it was through the flesh, God did..." (Rom. 8:3 NAS). In other words, I could not respond to the law because the law was limited by what I was able to do. The law says, "This do and thou shalt live." Since I found I could not do it, I died. You might as well tell a dog to fly. He just does not have the machinery. How do we find the solution? "...God did: sending His own Son in the likeness of sinful flesh and as an offering for sin, He condemned sin in the flesh, in order that the requirement of the Law might be fulfilled in us..." (Rom. 8:3-4 NAS). I am no longer in the sphere of the flesh because the Spirit of Christ is in me.

The sphere of the flesh is the whole legalistic system; it is "the law of a carnal [fleshly] commandment" (Heb. 7:16). The believer has been freed from that sphere and is now in the sphere of the Spirit. The relationship is new and the basis of judgment is new. The law of the Spirit of life sets me free to be judged according to the life of Jesus Christ (see Rom. 8:2). In Jesus the Father finds no fault.

Not Without Fault

Although our walk is not without fault, it is a walk without the failure of God's purpose. The Lord Jesus is in us to make a success out of our failures.

For example, when Moses went to the rock the second time, he was angry and smote the rock instead of speaking to it as God said (see Num. 20:7-12). Was God angry with Moses? Of course He was. But did water come out of the rock anyhow? Of course it did. You see, God made a success of Moses' failure. We may do it all wrong, but God will cause it to turn out right.

This is His work we are engaged in and He intends it to succeed. Success comes not by works of righteousness on our part, but rather through the faithfulness of Him who called us. It is altogether the mercy of our Lord that brings about His desired end. If this were not true, there would be no possibility of succeeding in His purpose. Someone always expresses the concern that we are giving a license to act in an irresponsible manner. Granted, there are always those thoughts of self-will that want us to "do our own thing." How does God deal with them? Does He tell us what not to do? No. God deals with it on the basis of mutual love and respect. I choose not to commit an offense before God, because I have realized with what great love God has loved me. Thus Paul says, "For the love of Christ controls us" (2 Cor. 5:14 NAS). According to Paul, if we are "controlled," it is not because of anything anyone told us to do or not to do. We are controlled because we recognize that God loves us and we are being changed by His love. The more we grow in His love, the more His love constrains or controls us to do His will. Is not the real problem and tragedy that believers do not really seek the Lord? They do not hunger after righteousness and the Kingdom of God, which would bring change to their lives. Someone once said, "We will be most like what we most look at." Paul said, "But we all, with open face beholding as in a glass the glory of the Lord, are changed into the same image from glory to glory, even as by the Spirit of the Lord" (2 Cor. 3:18). Paul deals with the problem of self-effort in Romans 7: "For the good that I wish, I do not do; but I practice the very evil that I do not wish...Who will set me free from the body of this death?" (Rom. 7:19,24 NAS) It is important to recognize that we want to walk uprightly before the Lord. Anyone serious enough about his relationship with God to read this book wants to walk right. But each of us discovers that we do not walk right all of the time.

On the one hand we have the "old man," the man who existed before we were born again. When we were born again, God did a most remarkable thing. He separated us from the old man and caused its death. "...our old self was crucified with Him, that our body of sin might be done away with..." (Rom. 6:6 NAS). Only three times in the New Testament does the phrase "old man" occur, and there only in Paul's epistles. Each time the old man is inactive; he is dead. Since he is dead, Paul tells us to put off the old man (see Eph. 4:22). So the problem that remains is our flesh. We act out of our flesh and not out of our regenerated spirit. The key to the focus of our desire, whether flesh or spirit, is what we choose to do. Our choice indicates if our desire is toward the Lord. Paul said he did not want to do the wrong thing, so his desire was toward the Lord. God wants all of His sons to have a similar heart after Him.

A classic illustration of this truth is David's heart. David had a heart after God, yet we know he was not without sin. Nevertheless, God covered David with His grace, since his heart was after Him. So it is with the believer today. When we commit an offense against the Lord by doing wrongly, our heart is grieved. When we confess our wrong, we need to remember that God has already reckoned this offense to the old man who died on the cross with Christ.

"But if I do the very thing I do not wish to do, I agree with the Law, confessing that it is good" (Rom. 7:16 NAS). I agree with the law because I really did not want to do it. "So now, no longer am I the one doing it, but sin which indwells me" (Rom. 7:17 NAS). As I mentioned earlier, the singular word *sin* in the New Testament indicates the root or the old man, whereas the word *sins* in the plural indicates the fruit that is the activity of the flesh. Thus Paul says, "So now, no longer am I the one doing it, but sin which indwells me. For I know that nothing good dwells in me, that is, in my flesh..." (Rom. 7:17-18 NAS). There is no good in the old man whom God has already crucified. When I sin, (remember, frequency is immaterial), God has already separated me from the sin and said that I did not do it. When I do what I do not want to do, I must immediately agree with God, "Lord, it was not me who did it. It was sin dwelling in me." One might ask, "Does not that encourage one not to care and go on in sin?" That question misses the point. We do not want to sin. Our desire to walk uprightly does not waver all the time. God is creating a people "zealous of good works." He is creating a people who have a heart toward Him and His righteousness. That is His goal. He will have success in it. (See First Thessalonians 5:23-24).

His Ways

There are many things we do not yet see as God sees them. For example, when I was first born again, I knew it was wrong to *speak* unkindly to a brother, but I did not know that it was wrong *to think* unkindly toward him. I thought that as long as I did not say it, I was all right. Then God began to show me that thinking unkindly was as bad as speaking unkindly. As a matter of fact, it was even worse, for it was deceitful. Sin is deceitful. There was no problem until He showed me that He did not like my attitude. God shows us these things as our relationship grows in His love and as our intimacy, awareness, and knowledge of Him grows. Then the closer we get to Him, the more He is able to make us aware of those things of which He disapproves. However, He does not show them to us until we are ready to respond by correcting the problem. Otherwise, it brings condemnation without correction.

Someone might say, "I knew bad thoughts were wrong and I was not condemned." But you did feel guilt because of a quickened spirit. You had no conviction because you did not yet see as God sees. There is a difference between guilt and conviction. We must see our wrong *condition* before we can see our right *position*.

> *He who did not spare His own Son, but delivered Him up for us all, how will He not also with Him freely give us all things? ... Who is the one who condemns? Christ Jesus is He who died, yes, rather who was raised, who is at the right hand of God, who also intercedes for us* (Romans 8:32,34 NAS).

The One who has justified us will not be the one to condemn us. He waits until we are mature enough to respond to His higher standard. Then He shows us the dark area of our soul in His light. By then we want to rise to fill His desire. Still, we will fail even after we choose His better way.

What God wants us to understand is that His love is not diminished. He reminds the convicted saint that it was not he who failed, but the sin that dwells in him. God does not reckon that failure to our account. He has imputed that to Christ on the tree and it is done away in Christ. If we sin the same sin a hundred times in one day and confess it every time as something we do not choose, then the last time we sin is the first time He saw it. All other times were wiped away by the blood. You may say to Him, "Lord, I did it again." His reply may well be, "Did what again?"

Now, this does not really release us to "do our own thing." What it does is make us conscious that there is a new motivation inside us toward the righteousness of God. We will still, on our own, never accomplish that righteousness of God apart from His life in us. You might well ask, since we are "predestined to become conformed to the image of His Son" (Rom. 8:29), why He does not just "zap" us and straighten us all out at once. The reason is so He can raise us up in Himself, so He can mature us, teach us of Himself and teach us to totally depend upon Him. It also allows us to be so involved in the process that we truly rejoice at the progress we make as He creates, for Himself, "safe sons."

Learning About Ourselves

Israel wandered for 40 years in the wilderness so they could learn about themselves—so Israel could know Israel. They had an opportunity to learn about God, but they did not want to learn. So God had to teach them about themselves. Likewise, the only way we will want to learn anything about the Lord is to discover how badly we need Him. When we discover how badly we need Him, then we will want to turn to Him. We will not turn to Him as long as we think we are sufficient on our own. Paul said, "Not that we are adequate in ourselves to consider anything as coming from ourselves, but our adequacy is from God" (2 Cor. 3:5 NAS). When we learn that, then God can ready give us the "spirit of wisdom and revelation in the knowledge of Him" (Eph. 1:17). One time a dear Christian lady came to me for ministry, saying she had a problem that had plagued her for a number of years. She had done everything she could to overcome it. She had dedicated her life to conquer it, she had used will power; she had prayed herself and been prayed for by others. She went on and on through a whole gamut of her efforts. I sensed, during the course of her conversation, what might be hindering her. I asked her, "Tell me something, dear sister. Why do you want to be rid of the problem?" She said, "Well, it is sin. I don't want to be sinning." I said, "How do you suppose God feels about that?" She answered, "Well, I am sure *He* does not like it." I asked, "Would you be willing to keep the sin and let God be your righteousness?" She nearly fell off the piano bench where she was sitting. "Are you willing to stay a sinner and let God be the only righteousness you have?"

You see, the sin was not bothering the Lord. It was bothering her. It bothered her because it made her look bad. She was not so concerned that it was interrupting her spiritual growth, or that it might be grieving the heart of her Lord. Rather she was concerned that it made her look bad before other believers. God wanted her to know that He was satisfied with her the way she was, sin and all. She was trying to be righteous in the eyes of everyone else. God wanted to make her understand that she never would be righteous. Rather she would have to rejoice in the cross and not in her own behavior or her own flesh (see Gal. 6:13).

Just as there are those who, through their legalistic ways, would put us under bondage so they can "glory in your flesh," so we do the same thing to ourselves in order that we might glory in our own flesh. There are vast numbers of believers who rejoice in their own behavior. "I do not do those sinful things," they are quick to tell you. Is that not a good example of self-righteousness and religious pride? "Which say, stand by thyself, come not near to me; for I am holier than thou" (Is. 65:5).

God has already paid for sin and has put it away "as far as the east is from the west" (Ps. 103:12). He is not concerned with the sin itself. He is concerned with how that sin interrupts our relationship with Him and our spiritual growth. Love covers a multitude of sin (see 1 Pet. 4:8), so sin is not the problem. The problem lies in our attitude. The flesh in us has been trained by the old man and the flesh wants to survive. God is renewing our minds so we don't think with the mind of the flesh any longer. The renewed mind is the mind of the Spirit. So when we sin, we must recognize that it is not us, but sin that dwells in us. If we do not recognize this truth, we will come under condemnation and walk in a living death. Thus we receive guilt when we do not agree with the finished work of Christ. "There is therefore now no condemnation for those who are in Christ Jesus"

(Rom. 8:1 NAS). This is the same as Romans 7:17. We have been educated in the Scripture to understand that when God repeats anything, it is vitally important, and we need to get hold of what He is saying.

To understand God in this matter is to know you are released from condemnation. To be released from condemnation is to be released from the guilt that destroys. The believer who fails to understand this vital part of Paul's gospel has arrested his spiritual growth and may walk in despair. We will only be able to grow as we mature in the liberty we find in Christ. Where there is a legal restraint placed on us, there will be no liberty and, therefore, no growth. "For the law made nothing perfect..." (Heb. 7:19). This is the "bottom line" of Paul's gospel.

Chapter 7

The Church
and Her Mission

Paul wrote 13 of the books in the New Testament. Four were letters addressed to individuals and nine were letters addressed to churches. Each of his letters (epistles) had a basic theme. In the personal letters the themes were the following:

1 Timothy—The House of God
2 Timothy—The Man of God
Titus—The Works of God
Philemon—The Imputation of God

In each of Paul's epistles to the local assemblies (churches) runs a theme about establishing the believer's relationship in Christ. The overall theme of Paul's message is that the believer is *in Christ*. The outworking of this is *Christ in us*. This is what Jesus was pointing toward when He spoke of the advent of the Holy Spirit: "Ye in Me, and I in you" (Jn. 14:20). Therefore, in each church letter is an underlying message for the Body of Christ as a whole, which defines our position as we are—*in Christ*:

Romans—In Christ, Justified
1 Corinthians—In Christ, Sanctified
2 Corinthians—In Christ, Comforted
Galatians—In Christ, Crucified
Ephesians—In Christ, In the Heavenlies
Philippians—In Christ, Satisfied
Colossians—In Christ, Complete
1 Thessalonians—In Christ, Translated
2 Thessalonians—In Christ, Vindicated

When we put all of these together, we have a complete picture of what God has done for man in the cross and the resurrection of the Lord Jesus Christ. The order of these accomplished works is important also. Our liberty is directly related from one work to the other. For example, we do not enjoy complete liberty if we are not satisfied that He is satisfied. Our concern at this point is with the message to the saints in Galatia, that every believer in Christ Jesus walk in the liberty provided through His finished work.

The Things of Christ

The four Gospels provide us with a view of the life and words of our Savior. The Gospels are popular because they provide material for preaching and teaching about Jesus. But Jesus said that after He sent the Holy Spirit, the Spirit would take the things of Christ and show them to us. This is why we have the epistles. They are the message of the Spirit to us through the apostles, telling us more about Jesus. The Gospels are the introduction of the Kingdom of God. To live only on a diet of the Gospels is to be in spiritual anemia.

The epistles tell us how the Kingdom works in practical terms. When that message is corrupted, the image of Christ in the Church also is corrupted. We have emphasized the uniqueness of Paul's writings. In defense of his own writings Paul says, "...do I seek to please men? for if I yet pleased men, I should not be the servant of Christ" (Gal. 1:10). The difficulty Paul faced was the result of the completely new message he was preaching. From God's perspective, there was nothing new about it. It was new for people. Was the Church a new thing or a part of God's plan? Did He decide, at the last minute, that He would call out of the Gentiles a people for His name and a bride for His Son? Was it only after Israel's failure that He "dumped" them and started again with the Gentiles? How absurd to think this could be so! The Church, the bride of Christ, was in the plan of God from the foundations of the world.

To begin with, God looked out over the nations of the world and chose Israel for His wife (see Is. 54:5). From this wife He begat a Son, whom He named Jesus. For that Son, the Father is now calling out of the Gentiles a bride, the Church, which is His Body. We are bone of His bone and flesh of His flesh (see Eph. 5:25-32). "According as He hath chosen us in Him before the foundation of the world...And hath put all things under His feet, and gave Him to be the head over all things to the church, which is His body, the fulness of Him that filleth all in all" (Eph. 1:4,22-23). The Scripture is filled with illustrations telling us that God's purpose was first of all to call Israel as the wife of Jehovah, then, while she is put away in blindness for her adultery, to call the Gentiles as a bride for His Son. This is magnificently portrayed in the wife God fashioned for Adam.

Paul said that the first Adam was a figure or type of the last Adam (see Rom. 5:14). God made man without the aid of woman. For man He made a woman by opening the side of Adam and from his bone creating a "help meet." The wife of the man disobeyed the command of God and stood, with the forbidden fruit in hand, offering it to her husband. He might have said, "You foolish woman, do you realize what you have done?" But no, without a word, like a sheep before its shearers is silent, he took of the fruit and ate. Why? He loved that woman.

I have been told that God would have given him another mate. Adam did not want another; he wanted that one. He loved her with an untainted love like unto that which God had for him. That was the only kind of love that Adam knew. He wanted to keep the woman God had created for him. How could he do that? The only way was to die with her. He knew God's love for him was as great as his love for her, and that God would find a way. So he ate of the fruit and they both died. After God had exposed their iniquity, He made coats of skins and clothed them. Now, I do not mean to diminish the tragedy of the fall, but it is important to point out God's love as we see it in this passage.

Is this not what Jesus did for us? Without a word of complaint, He went to the cross and from His pierced side His bride was born. "...Except a corn of wheat fall into the ground and die, it abideth alone: but if it die, it bringeth forth much fruit" (Jn. 12:24). Jesus Christ "loved the church, and gave Himself for it" (Eph. 5:25). Jesus loved the Church, His bride, and was willing to die to keep her. Now we are joined to the Lord and our spirit is one with Him (see 1 Cor. 6:17). Our entire relationship with Him is like a Bridegroom and His bride. The message of this relationship was in danger of being corrupted by the legalists from Jerusalem. This, Paul could not abide.

Paul was not preaching anything foreign to the eternal purposes of God, but it seemed that way to the legalists. In their opinion, Paul had departed from the doctrines of Moses. In reality, he was preaching the fulfillment of the law of Moses. Their eyes were blinded to the greater message of the law (see 2 Cor. 3:14). The Church was in God's plan from before time began, but it was a mystery hidden in ages past. Now it was being revealed through the preaching of the apostles, Paul having received the greater message of the grace of God. Because they could not see God's complete design, though, they began to persecute the apostle Paul severely.

According to Paul, they did not persecute him because they were particularly zealous of the law. "Those who desire to make a good showing in the flesh try to compel you to be circumcised, simply that they may not be persecuted for the cross of Christ" (Gal. 6:12 NAS). The law dealt with all that was outward and fleshly. Paul viewed his antagonists, who were pressing him to conform to the law, as more concerned with making a good showing in the flesh to avoid persecution. Galatians 5:11 deals with much the same problem: "But I, brethren, if I still preach circumcision, why am I still persecuted? Then the stumbling block of the cross has been abolished" (NAS).

The Greek word for "offense" is *skandalon*, from which we get our word *scandal*. Paul was pointing out there would be no offense if he were to interject a bit of law in his message. "If I preached circumcision, then there would not be any scandal in the cross. If I would just intermingle a bit of law in this, then there would be no offense." Beloved, the same thing that made the cross offensive then, makes the cross offensive now. The cross completely eliminates me and gives an accurate assessment of what I am. Let us face it, the flesh does not want to see itself crucified. The philosophy of man-invented religion is that I will do a little, God will do a little, and between the two of us, we will get together. I repeat the words of the Mormon: "Jesus made the down payment and now we must keep up the payments." What a hopeless philosophy. When you are totally bankrupt, you need someone who both can and will pay off your debt. Jesus did this for all who come to Him by faith in the finished work of the cross.

> *For those who are circumcised do not even keep the Law themselves, but they desire to have you circumcised, that they may boast in your flesh. But may it never be that I should boast, except in the cross of our Lord Jesus Christ, through which the world has been crucified to me, and I to the world* (Galatians 6:13-14 NAS).

The circumcised did not keep the law, but they wanted the Galatian believers to be identified with them. When everyone is in the same boat, there is a false sense of comfort. Also, the legalists could enjoy a measure of carnal joy because they were successful in putting the Galatians under the law with them.

This is like the old adage, "If I am not happy, I do not want anyone else to be happy either. If I am not walking in liberty, I do not want anyone else walking in liberty either. If my religion is miserable, then I want everybody else to have a miserable religion." When I accept what I am and what God in Christ has done through the cross on my behalf without adding anything else, then all of the legalistic philosophies of man-established religion, including many Christian religions, will come to persecute me. The cross causes a scandal because it eliminates "us" from making a contribution of redeeming value. All that is left is God, who ministers His grace on our behalf. Those who have not found peace in that message will add to it and be resentful of anyone who contradicts their position.

Paul says, "If I were still trying to please men, I would not be a bond-servant of Christ" (Gal. 1:10b NAS). Paul is not out to please men; neither did God call preachers to be popular. He called them to be honest, to tell the truth, and to speak the truth in love, but not to be popular. Paul was declaring that since he was to be the servant of Christ, he had settled in his mind that not everyone would agree with what he had to say.

If we look at the character of the Lord Jesus Christ, we see His longsuffering, His compassion, His loving kindness, His gentleness, and His tenderness. We assume that when the Body of Christ displays these qualities, the world will embrace Him and people will be converted. Beloved, if we see people converted, it will not be because we have presented the marvelous characteristics of Christ in our walk. People are converted because the gospel of Christ is the power of God unto salvation to them that believe (see Rom. 1:16). When we introduce them to Jesus Christ and exalt Him as our Lord and the Redeemer of sinners, conversion will take place. It won't take place because we are being sweet to everyone we meet.

Jesus presented Himself as He was to the Jewish people of His day, and to the Pharisees in particular.

What they saw was a complete and true picture of Him and of the Father. How did they receive Him? They hated Him. "We will not have this man reign over us!" as the parable says (Lk. 19:14). When I examine the record of Jesus' life, I find no one more capable of reigning over me. The Pharisees, however, did not want Him to reign over them. Why? Legalism always rejects righteousness. Justice is never befriended by rebellion. The world never embraces the goodness of God because the world is not looking for goodness. The world is looking for anarchy and it uses an evil imagination to go the way of an unredeemed heart.

If a lost man could manage to "get into the presence of God—the glory of God," he would be utterly miserable. If a lost man could go to Heaven, it would be hell to him. The light would show him up for what he really is. The believer faces the same glorious light when he is convicted by the Holy Spirit—the light reveals what he is. At that point he has two options: either he can react in rebellion or he can react in submission.

Cain was faced with the righteousness of his brother. Abel was willing to confess he was a sinner and needed a substitute sacrifice. Cain's response to Abel's blood offering was to kill Abel. We see that theme repeated again and again. This same spirit in the Pharisees caused them to deal with Jesus in the same way. The world is not being won by the message of a compassionate, loving, tender, gentle Jesus.

All manner of religions declare Him to be all of these and more. Only when the Holy Spirit goes forth and convicts the sinner of his sin, of righteousness, and of judgment to come, will conversions result. That is the only way anyone is ever converted to Christ.

Example or Message

Our tendency to get sentimental when we preach the gospel of the God of Love is a concern. Perhaps we are trying to preach the gospel by example when that is not the correct method. The preaching of the gospel is not by example, but by the Spirit of God. As the Spirit of God ministers the Word of God, people will be convicted and convert to the righteousness of God.

I am not saying that believers ought not walk in the character of Christ. To the contrary, He is our goal (see Phil. 3). That, however, is not something to be decided by will power. Neither is it imitation; it is habitation. It is the presence of the character and the life of Jesus Christ in us that causes others to react to Jesus in either a positive or a negative way. Paul makes a most important statement in this connection in Second Corinthians 2:14-17.

Now thanks be unto God, which always causeth us to triumph in Christ, and maketh manifest the savour of His knowledge by us in every place. For we are unto God a sweet savour of Christ, in them that are saved, and in them that perish: to the one we are the savour of death unto death; and to the other the savour of life unto life. And who is sufficient for these things? For we are not as many, which corrupt the word of God: but as of sincerity, but as of God, in the sight of God speak we in Christ (2 Corinthians 2:14-17).

The seed you sow must be the pure Word of God. The fruit of that seed will be determined by the ground in which it falls, not by the quality of the seed. If the way we portray Him is consistent, we will see two types of reactions: those who submit to the righteous claims of Christ and those who will not. Remember Paul said, "If I were still trying to please men, I would not be a bond-servant of Christ" (Gal 1:10b NAS). If everyone patted Paul on the back and said, "Paul, you are doing a fine job. I really appreciate what you are doing," Paul would start looking himself over to find out what he was doing wrong. Jesus said, "Woe unto you, when all men shall speak well of you" (Lk. 6:26a). If a man is to be a servant of God, he will not be popular in the world. That is the effect of the Truth in the worlds of both religion and paganism. Those who embrace the Truth, rather than the traditions of man, are esteemed by God.

Hebrews 13 gives us an excellent example of the law anticipating those who would reject grace. "Wherefore Jesus also, that He might sanctify the people with His own blood, suffered without the gate. Let us go forth therefore unto Him without the camp, bearing His reproach" (Heb. 13:12-13). Under the law, sacrifices were carried outside the camp and burned. They did so because the camp was holy and the sacrifice became, on their behalf, unholy. There the defiled (unholy) could avail himself of the sacrifice and then come back into the holy camp. Over the years, the holy camp deteriorated into a religious exercise. When Jesus Christ came, He was the perfect sacrifice showing them a shadow or figure of what was to come. Jesus was sacrificed outside the camp (city). Because the holy camp had deteriorated into a religious exercise, He was rejected. The righteous One who was the only one capable of cleansing all within the camp fits the description in Hebrews 13:10: "We have an altar, from which those who serve the tabernacle have no right to eat" (NAS). Who is referred to in "those who serve the tabernacle"? The writer is referring to the religious exercise of Judaism, saying that we have an altar from which they have no right to eat. They eat at a religious altar, and we eat at a living altar, an altar of life. It is an altar for living sacrifices.

"For the bodies of those beasts, whose blood is brought into the sanctuary by the high priest for sin, are burned without the camp" (Heb. 13:11). There is a reproach for those who would be identified with Jesus. You are outside the camp of traditional religion, which is based on works and self-effort. (Sadly, this camp includes many well-meaning Christians who do not know the liberty of the cross.) A good example of this reproach is seen when the disciples began to minister in the name of Jesus of Nazareth. They were laying hands on the sick and the sick were being healed. Did the Sanhedrin command them to stop laying on hands and healing? No. They did not care what the disciples did so long as they did not "do it in the name of Jesus" (see Acts 4). "You can go on healing people; that is good. We need to help the sick, but do not speak or preach in His name." It was the name of Jesus that brought their objections. Today, we can talk about "the man upstairs"; "the good Lord"; and even "God" for that matter and people will, with few exceptions, not be offended. But as soon as the name "Jesus" is mentioned, the whole conversation becomes tense and people get fidgety and nervous. There is something about His name that causes revolt in the religious as well as the worldly. It is a proclamation of "one Way religion."

Revelation

> *But I certify you, brethren, that the gospel which was preached of me is not after man. For I neither received it of man, neither was I taught it, but by the revelation of Jesus Christ* (Galatians 1:11-12).

What can we learn about this "revelation" Paul is speaking of here? In an earlier chapter we discussed the parallel between Paul and Moses and the unique authority of these two men. Here the Spirit assures us that Paul was teaching and writing the word of the Lord.

For this cause I Paul, the prisoner of Jesus Christ for you Gentiles, if ye have heard of the dispensation of the grace of God which is given me to you-ward: ... Which in other ages was not made known unto the sons of men, as it is now revealed unto His holy apostles and prophets by the Spirit; that the Gentiles should be fellow-heirs, and of the same body, and partakers of His promise in Christ by the gospel (Ephesians 3:1-2,5-6).

These truths were new to the Jews who heard this message because they were hidden in the Old Testament record. Unless someone interpreted the hidden meaning, their search for meaning was futile. Paul was taken into the heavens to be taught by God of these mysteries of the things to come. Paul and the other apostles give us God's revelation of these hidden truths in their epistles. God makes the unknown, known.

Illumination

At the same time, God opens our understanding as He did the disciples' (see Lk. 24:45). He wants to increase our understanding of what has been revealed. Jesus gave thanks to the Father for the ability He gives to hear truth. "...I thank Thee, O Father, Lord of heaven and earth, because Thou hast hid these things from the wise and prudent, and hast revealed them unto babes" (Mt. 11:25). The Scripture asks the question, "Can a man, by searching, find out about God?" (see Job 11:7) The obvious answer is, "no." For all the effort a student may put into study, he will only see the truths of God by the light of the Holy Spirit. Paul confirms this in First Corinthians 1:21: "For after that in the wisdom of God the world by wisdom knew not God, it pleased God by the foolishness of preaching to save them that believe." Do you think it strange that educated men know a great deal about the Word of God, but not know the God of the Word? On the other hand, some fellow with little or no education, who receives his Bible education at home, understands the truth of God and the God of Truth. Can you know Scripture by sweat and labor? No. Really knowing Scripture comes through "the spirit of wisdom and revelation in the knowledge of Him" (Eph. 1:17).

Many years ago, while I was in college, a dear Italian brother came to speak in our chapel service. He had come to this country when he was 16 years old. In his testimony he told how he was a drunken altar boy and how he stumbled into a basement church in New England where they were singing "The Old Rugged Cross." The Lord marvelously saved him, and he grew wonderfully in the grace and knowledge of Jesus Christ. He read the Scripture in many languages: English, Italian, French, and, as I now recall, German. In the course of one of his many messages to us, he made a comment that I have never forgotten. This Italian gentleman said, "Beloved, I'm-a never read-a this-a book. You-a never read-a this-a book. This-a book's-a gotta be-a read-a to you!" What a profound but simple truth. If God, by His Spirit, is not communicating His Word to us as we read, then our understanding is unfruitful.

Do not misunderstand, God is not pleased with continued ignorance. It is our responsibility to study all we can about the Word of God. It is true Paul said there were "not many wise" called, but he did not say there were not *any* wise called (see 1 Cor. 1:26). I was always grateful for learned men to read behind. Many in the Body of Christ would benefit if they stopped insisting, "God teaches me His Word," and start availing themselves of what God has taught other men of faith. (See Proverbs 22:17-21.)

Letter or Spirit

The New Testament age is one of the Spirit and not of the letter of the law. In the New Testament these two opposing concepts are expressed by the words *spirit* and *flesh*. The *spirit* addresses all that is in the new life in Christ Jesus and the *flesh* is the old sphere of the law and its weakness. These two words are used together in Romans 8:1 and Romans 8:4 in that very sense. Paul tells us that people are in one or the other of these two spheres depending on regeneration. Those who are born again are in the sphere of the spirit and those who are not born again are in the sphere of the flesh. Romans 8:9 makes the distinction and is the key to this chapter. To walk after the flesh is not a reference to our behavior, but to the old system and its demands. We who are in

Christ are in the economy of the Spirit of Christ and are not subject to the bondage that accompanied the old system.

Paul admitted that he excelled under the old system. According to Galatians 1:14, he advanced in Judaism more than all his peers. However, in Philippians 3:8, he counts all that he had gained as a loss to Christ. Even though he was righteous under the sphere, or economy, of the law, he produced no gain before God. Flesh (law) is a self-activity, while spirit is the flow of the life of the indwelling Christ. Like the difference between life and death, these two systems are so different that to mix the two brought severe rebuke from the great apostle. The church at Philippi was being infected by those who were zealous for the law, sowing diverse seed in their field and so defiling them.

In Philippians 3:2 Paul refers to such men as "dogs" and "evil workers." He even uses a word the King James Version translates as "concision," which some scholars have translated as "mutilators." Dogs were unclean animals to an Israelite. The people were not prone to keep dogs as pets, since they were associated with the ravenous beasts of the field. Gentiles, though, kept them for pets. Jesus referred to the Syrophoenician woman as a dog when she cried out, "Have mercy on me, O Lord, Thou son of David." In her answer she said, "Truth, Lord: yet the dogs eat of the crumbs which fall from their masters' table." She practiced the "truth" by immediately agreeing with the law, then she asked for mercy and grace. Jesus' reply was, "O woman, great is thy faith: be it unto thee even as thou wilt." (See Matthew 15:22-28.) How marvelous is our Lord. In this event you can see the difference between the letter and the spirit. The letter of the law would not have allowed that woman to go away with anything because she was a Gentile and alienated from the commonwealth of Israel. But a spirit-led economy calls for the Spirit to dissolve the word into life in Jesus Christ. Jesus came to minister the Spirit. He said, "The words that I have spoken to you are spirit and are life" (Jn. 6:63b NAS). The Vine produces fruit by nature, not by command.

You can excel in religion by your zeal for the system and, before you know it, reach the pinnacle of your religious group.

Though I might also have confidence in the flesh. If any other man thinketh that he hath whereof he might trust in the flesh, I more: ... But what things were gain to me, those I counted loss for Christ (Philippians 3:4,7).

If it makes me look good, it makes Christ look bad. If my religious endeavor and exercise turn attention on me, then they turn people's attention away from the cross of Christ and from the power of His resurrection. Jesus puts it this way: "But he who practices the truth comes to the light, that his deeds may be manifested as having been wrought in God"

(Jn. 3:21 NAS). It is not, "he that does religion" nor "he that does righteousness" nor "he that does good work," but "he that does the truth." How does one "do" the truth? It is not just being obedient to the Word, which is Truth. It is being honest about who I am. It is being honest to the point of transparency about my failures and weaknesses. Then if any good fruit or work comes out of me, you know for sure it is the Lord.

King Saul and King David are both examples of this point. Saul was commanded to destroy all the Amalakites, but he decided to save their king and the best of the sheep and cattle. When confronted by the prophet Samuel, Saul said, "Yes, I have sinned, but honor me now before the people that I might sacrifice to the Lord." (See First Samuel 15.) He admitted his guilt, but wanted to be honored instead of honest. That is choosing darkness instead of light.

David, on the other hand, committed a sin considered to be far more dreadful in our eyes. He stole a man's wife, committed adultery, and sent the man to his death. David, like Saul, did not come forward on his own. He was confronted by the prophet Nathan. Nathan rebuked him, and in David's response lies the difference. (See Second Samuel 11–12.) In contrast to Saul, David confessed his sin and recorded his confession in Psalm 51 for Israel and all the world to read. He chose light instead of darkness. It is fair to ask, "Which of these two men did the truth;

which kept the crown?" Solomon tells us "He that covereth his sins shall not prosper: but whoso confesseth and forsaketh them shall have mercy" (Prov. 28:13). Light heals; darkness brings decay. The lost person is not interested in meeting a sinner who has become righteous. He needs the kind of mercy that will make righteous people out of sinners and the One who has the answer is the Savior, Jesus.

The Passive Witness

Jesus said, "You shall be My witnesses" (Acts 1:8 NAS), which means the believer is in the Lord's hand to accomplish His purpose. In a sense the believer in Christ is a passive witness to the world, for it is the Spirit who does the work of revealing Jesus to the world.

Now thanks be unto God, which always causeth us to triumph in Christ, and maketh manifest the savour of His knowledge by us in every place. For we are unto God a sweet savour of Christ, in them that are saved, and in them that perish: to the one we are the savour of death unto death; and to the other the savour of life unto life. And who is sufficient for these things? (2 Corinthians 2:14-16)

Even when the saint fails in a proper witness, the Lord is still able to use him to manifest His salvation. You will have an effect on those whom you meet, depending on the kind of "soil" they are. You will either be a testimony to judgment or you will be a savour of life. If they are stony ground, then death will confront them. If they are good ground, they will receive a message of hope. "Know ye not that ye are the temple of God, and that the Spirit of God dwelleth in you?" (1 Cor. 3:16) Where the Spirit of the Lord is, the message of His Person will be testifying of Jesus as the Christ. This message is not and cannot be hidden. If only the saints of the Lord could come to rest in Him, knowing "it is God which worketh in you both to will and to do of His good pleasure" (Phil. 2:13).

Dr. Harry Ironside was a former pastor of the Moody Memorial Church in Chicago. One time when he was on a tour through London, the group came to a certain industrial area. Dr. Ironside said, "What is that fragrance I smell?" His guide said to him, "Do you see those people coming out of that building over there? That is a perfume factory. All those people are breaking for lunch and they bear the fragrance of what they have been with all morning." Jesus is always with you and you bear His fragrance even though you may not be conscious of it. Those whom you come in contact with are aware of it. The world may respond favorably or unfavorably toward that fragrance. We must remember that we are not judges or prosecutors, only witnesses. Witnesses we will be and must be.

Chapter 8

The Futility of the Law

The law of Moses was based on outer restrictions. In dealing with Israel, God outlined a number of "Thou shalt, thou shalt not" commandments because the Holy Spirit had not yet been sent to witness of those things which God approved or disapproved. "...The Holy Ghost was not yet given; because that Jesus was not yet glorified" (Jn. 7:39). In this aspect, Paul's message was unique especially as it related to their position in liberty. The Holy Spirit brings peace with God and liberty, which derives its authority from the indwelling life of Christ. If the believer recognizes himself as moving by an inner motivation, then he does not need outer restrictions.

When the children of Israel came out of Egypt, they worshiped idols like the Egyptians did. Joshua said, "They served idols across the seas" (see Josh. 24). So when the people came out of the land of Egypt, they were introduced to Jehovah God for the first time. This was a new revelation. What little they remembered from the stories and experience of their fathers did not help them to realize their true calling. They probably retained some of their fathers' traditions, but those traditions fell far short of God's purpose for them.

Often the traditions we pass down to our children lose the real spiritual value they were intended to have. God has given us truths and we formed them into tradition. There are some rituals that are a part of some denominations—such as kneeling and standing during readings and prayers—that were started out of deep reverence for God and His Word. Now they are continued by rote and only because people are trained to observe the same tradition. The children of Israel felt secure as children of Abraham, but they no longer knew what that calling meant. Thus, they began to worship the idols of Egypt. Then, when God delivered them from bondage, He gave them a new revelation concerning Himself through Moses. That revelation was written and given to the people as the "Law of Moses."

The law was added to the promise so they could know what God approved and did not approve. That revelation was designed to last until the Seed would come. When Christ came, the law was made obsolete. This "outside" system for governing behavior proved to be inadequate and was unable to complete the task of bringing saints to maturity and the knowledge of God. It set limits for right and wrong actions, but it could not make them righteous. Someone said, "It is like looking in a mirror to discover that your face is dirty. It will not wash your face, but it will show you all of the dirt." The law reveals what is wrong with me, but it cannot correct the problem. "It was weak through the flesh" (Rom. 8:3).

Christ came in the likeness of sinful flesh and gave a new principle for righteousness. This principle was His indwelling life in the believer. This is confirmed in Paul's letter to the Philippians: "For it is God who is at work in you, both to will and to work for His good pleasure" (Phil. 2:13 NAS). In Paul's controversy with the Judaizers from Jerusalem, as well as with Christians who were not enjoying full freedom from the law, the issue was the grace of God. We can see this in Paul's opening to the Galatians: "I marvel that ye are so soon removed from Him that called you into the grace of Christ unto another gospel" (Gal. 1:6). It is worth emphasizing again: Any activity on my part that attempts to obtain God's favor or, for that matter, to keep it, frustrates the grace of God and becomes "another gospel."

Paul's Zeal

Obviously, Paul was not a passive man. He put his whole being into whatever he did. This was true of his life under the law as well as his ministry of the grace of God. Before his conversion, he persecuted the Church of God and tried to discredit and destroy it. He did so out of zeal for the Lord. Even though he thought he was serving God, in reality he was attempting to destroy God's plan. His zeal, Paul tells us, was the reason God chose him as an example of grace. God could have killed him, but He chose instead to redeem him. Once he changed directions, Paul could say, "I am a beggar telling other beggars where I have found bread." He found out that grace is "good news for bad people."

If we had been believers in Paul's day, we probably would have been praying for God to get that man out of the way. Someone must have been praying for God to save him. I doubt that anyone is ever born into the Kingdom apart from prayer. Any birth is accompanied by travail, and prayer is the travail of the souls. "...As soon as Zion travailed, she brought forth her children" (Is. 66:8). This is the way of the Lord and it is no doubt true of Paul as well. Paul went through a little travail on his own. On his way to Damascus, the Lord stopped him and spoke these words to him: "It is hard for you to kick against the goads" (Acts 26:14 NAS). Probably Paul had been goaded, especially since the stoning of Stephen. In any case, he had been goaded by the Holy Spirit for some time, so God called him by His grace. God does not call someone because he is good. He calls people because He loves them and has a purpose for them. The greatest antidote to cure a "self-worth" problem is to discover the Lord of Glory loves you and wants you for His own. So Paul said, "He called me by His grace" (see Gal. 1:15).

Christian Zeal for Law

In the early days the seat of the Church was in Jerusalem. Among the apostles, James was the main spokesman and set forth the decisions made by the elders. James is an interesting man. He and the other brethren of Jerusalem remained zealous for the law of Moses. When the apostle Paul came on the scene, Paul was zealous for the law, but not in a way that James and the others could comprehend. Paul was zealous for the law because it testified of Christ and, in Christ, he saw the law fulfilled. When Paul's message helped believers see the law fulfilled in Christ, it was no longer the taskmaster it had been. Paul revealed the Christ who was the end of the law for righteousness for all who would believe. This did not sit well with some of the "pillars" at Jerusalem. Halfway through the Book of Acts (see Acts 15:5), many continued to say that the law of Moses must be kept. We are like that today when we think we must have some kind of outer regulation. We are not willing to release ourselves or our brethren to the power and efficiency of the Person of the Holy Spirit who dwells within. We would rather return to weak and beggarly elements that did not work in the first place. Such restrictions cause us to be weak through the flesh because they give us some measure of carnal security.

"But when Cephas came to Antioch, I opposed him to his face, because he stood condemned" (Gal. 2:11 NAS). Peter was the apostle to the Jews and he

147

came out of the church at Jerusalem. Paul said, "I withstood Peter to his face even in front of all those people. For prior to the coming of certain men from James" (he did not say "from Jerusalem," but "from James"), "he used to eat with the Gentiles. But when they came, he began to withdraw and hold himself aloof, fearing the party of the circumcision" (see Gal. 1:12). Why did he say "from James"? James was zealous for the law. Peter had been breaking bread with the Gentiles, but when those came from James, he withdrew, separating himself. "And the rest of the Jews joined him in hypocrisy..." (Gal. 2:13 NAS). These are Christians, but Peter separated himself and went over and ate with the Jews.

Peter knew that God wanted to embrace and include the Gentiles in His plan of redemption (see Acts 10). In a vision from God, he saw a sheet let down with "all kinds of four-footed animals and crawling creatures of the earth and birds of the air" (Acts 10:12 NAS). (Unclean animals in the Scriptures were used as a metaphor to refer to the Gentile nations.) A voice said, "What God has cleansed, no longer consider unholy" (Acts 10:15 NAS). In this Peter understood that he was to do whatever God told him regarding the Gentiles. Peter was given the privilege of introducing the Gentiles to the gospel and giving them the key of the Kingdom. Later, when the Jewish Christians arrived in Antioch, he did not want to be identified with the Gentiles. He went over and identified himself with the Jews. Paul said, "Peter, you are a hypocrite."

The flesh is continually weak, even for a man like Peter, who was filled with the Spirit of God. Like you and me, Peter was a man with emotions and feelings. Left to our own way, we always fail. It is refreshing to note that our Father is always willing to forgive our weaknesses. He uses whomever He wishes; He has no perfect servants. Jesus, His perfect Son, dwells in imperfect people to represent the perfect God as the One who will receive these imperfect people.

The End of the Law

James and the other "pillars" of the Church were faced with an important decision when they confronted the pure grace of God. They thought they had to abandon something God required. Their ties to the tradition through their cultural system was their whole life. Until Paul had his dramatic conversion, the same difficulty lay before him.

James, the brother of Jesus, appears in three important events in the Book of Acts. In Acts 12, he is with the brethren at Rhoda's house when they learn of Peter's release from prison. James appears again as the leader of the council in Jerusalem in Acts 15:13. Out of this council James issues four legal stipulations concerning the Gentiles: "Abstain from things contaminated by idols, from fornication, from what is strangled, and from blood" (see Acts 15:20 NAS). James, with the approval of the other elders, agree in the requirements. Acts 21:20 says, "they are all zealous for the Law" (NAS). Why did the brethren at Jerusalem fail to oppose this zeal for the law of their Jewish Christian brothers? They really did not want to do anything about it. They let the Jews, who were being converted in Jerusalem, continue in their zeal for the law. In their zeal, they were still devoted to what had "waxed" old and was ready to be done away. In Jerusalem, Paul was known for his efforts to set people free from the law. "They will certainly hear that you have come" (Acts 21:22b NAS). It is easy to see why this doctrinal conflict caused a problem between the Church in Jerusalem and the Church at Antioch. Those in Jerusalem asked, "Why would God do away with something so important as the law, which He had Himself given to His people?" For them it was a moral and cultural dilemma.

Purpose of the Law

Without proper guidelines, the concern is how to constrain the people and encourage right behavior. A reasonable question is whether or not any legal restraint should be required of God's people to create responsibility for maintaining a life of righteousness. I want to assure you, dear saint, that we do not have any problem in the Body of Christ today that they did not have in the early days of the Church. If a law could have corrected these problems, it would have been employed. The only reason the law was given, was to provide us with a schoolmaster. When Paul provided instructions in giving, he appeals to the law. "Thou shalt not muzzle the ox that treadeth out the corn" (1 Tim. 5:18). There is no threat or penalty with that. He is simply stating the principle of giving. In dealing with the immorality in Corinth, Paul said, "Shall I then take the members of Christ, and make them the members of an harlot?" (see 1 Cor. 6:15) He could have appealed to them with the seventh commandment, but instead He appeals to their union in the Body of Christ and the sanctity of that union. The very moment we impose a legalistic stipulation on the believer, we have built again the same system we had destroyed and so make ourselves transgressors (see Gal. 2:18). Paul tells us, "For Christ is the end of the law for righteousness to every one that believeth" (Rom. 10:4).

Paul is still speaking in the context of his conversation with Peter when he says this in Galatians 2:15-16:

> We who are Jews by nature, and not sinners of the Gentiles, knowing that a man is not justified by the works of the law, but by the faith of Jesus Christ, even we have believed in Jesus Christ, that we might be justified by the faith of Christ, and not by the works of the law: for by the works of the law shall no flesh be justified (Galatians 2:15-16).

Paul is not suggesting that Jews were not sinners personally, but that judicially they had a unique place before God. When they received Christ, they were at the same time acknowledging the inadequacy of the law to produce righteousness.

"But if, while we seek to be justified by Christ, we ourselves also are found sinners, is therefore Christ the minister of sin? God forbid" (Gal. 2:17). In referring to the Jews, he says that as a people they were not sinners in the same way as the Gentiles. As Jews, they believed Gentiles needed to get right with God, put away their wickedness, repent, and walk in righteousness. Proselyte after proselyte to Judaism was evidence that Gentiles were coming into the faith. Gentile conversion was not new to the Jews, but to insert another step in the process of salvation was news to them. In their view, they were born right the first time. The message of a Messiah who had to die in order for them to have life, staggered them. The law concluded all under sin, Jew and Gentile alike, that all might come to righteousness through faith in Jesus Christ (see Gal. 3:22). The message of the law was sin and sacrifice, imputation and death, and righteousness through a substitute. Jesus Christ is the person and the realization of all that the law prophesied. The purpose of the law was to declare the whole world and all that were in it to be under the bondage of sin. Jesus Christ was the sole solution to the world's condition. With His sacrifice, the law was no longer needed.

A Satisfied Witness

The law required not only a substitute in death, but also an imputation for life. Our sin had to be imputed to a substitute and the righteousness of the substitute had to be imputed to us. I remind you of the three great imputations in the Scripture: the imputation of the sin of Adam to the human race; the sin of the human race to Christ; and the righteousness of Christ to those who believe. These are illustrated through the law. So Paul said, "For through the Law I died to the Law, that I might live to God" (Gal. 2:19 NAS). The law prophesied that we were going to die. When it had finished its work, we had no need of it. It simply was a vehicle whereby God revealed our sinful condition and let us know what He would do to establish righteousness. When God had finished everything the law called for, it became obsolete. The Book of Hebrews confirms this: "When He said, 'A new covenant,' He has made the first obsolete. But whatever is becoming obsolete and growing old is ready to disappear" (Heb. 8:13 NAS).

Jesus is the end of the law and the fulfillment of it. If you fulfill a debt, you do not owe it anymore. Paul said, "I am through with the law, dead to the law." God had built into the law a self-destructive feature, so that when it was finished, or accomplished, it no longer stood over the believer. Righteousness has no foundation or part in the law. The law will not work to make one righteous now any more than it did before the cross. "For if I rebuild what I have once destroyed, I prove myself to be a transgressor" (Gal. 2:18 NAS).

The Law a Witness

The righteousness of God, apart from the law, is witnessed by the law and the prophets. How many witnesses does God require? "By the mouth of two or three witnesses every fact may be confirmed" (Mt. 18:16b NAS). "But now the righteousness of God without the law is manifested, being witnessed by the law and the prophets" (Rom. 3:21). So the law on one side and the prophets on the other witness this work of justice in the cross. The psalmist wrote: "Mercy and truth are met together; righteousness and peace have kissed each other. Truth shall spring out of the earth; and righteousness shall look down from heaven" (Ps. 85:10-11). Mercy and truth met together at Calvary.

This is the truth of God: We are sinners and we deserve judgment. God imputes our sin to His Son and mercy instantly appears. Mercy and truth have kissed each other at the cross, and righteousness and peace have sprung out of the earth. The Son of Man rises out of the earth, made in the form of sinful flesh, the last Adam from the dust of the earth to become the Lord from Heaven. The last Adam, who is also the second Man, has satisfied all that was required by the law and the prophets. The law required death. So the law looks down and says, "I am satisfied. I have poured out my wrath. I have vented my judgment, and I have vented it upon the One that God provided." In the same way, throughout the Old Testament, every offering that was presented, was presented with a view toward the Lord Jesus. Every offering became a substitute for wrath, like the animal that Abel put on the altar before God.

The law looked down from Heaven and said, "I witness to that. I am satisfied. I have vented my judgment." The prophets looked at Jesus and said, "He did it just like we said it must be done. Nothing was left out. This is God's Son, the only One who could fulfill the law." The prophets said, "We agree. That is the truth of God." The law said, "I agree. That is the order of God." So the law and the prophets have now become God's two "witnesses," the proof that the law is satisfied. God rests in the peace that He has obtained through the performance of His Word. Redeemed man and God are not at war anymore. "Therefore being justified by faith, we have peace with God through our Lord Jesus Christ" (Rom. 5:1). The war is over! Hallelujah!

If I go back to the law now and set up a legalistic ritual, I would be starting the war all over again. God is satisfied and whatever I do will not change Him. To refuse to accept that God is satisfied leaves us without peace with God. We will never enjoy the peace *of* God until we "cease from [our] own works, as God did from His" (see Heb. 4:10). There is no difference between Jew and Gentile, for all have sinned and, as a result, continually come short of His glory (see Rom. 3:22-23). It is important to note the way Paul states this fact. He says, "have sinned," which implies completed action. The sin of the first man, Adam, was in the past and his act was our act. Both Jew and Gentile are descendants of Adam, which is why Paul can say "all" in reference to sin. As a result, we continually fall short of the glory of God. Even with the law of Moses, we fell short of the glory of God. The law points out that we come short of the glory of God, and therefore it stands to condemn us. "For if I build again the things which I destroyed [dissolved], I make myself a transgressor" (Gal. 2:18). What then is the solution? "Being justified freely by His grace through the redemption that is in Christ Jesus" (Rom. 3:24).

If you want to continue transgressing, set up the law and you can have your wants fulfilled. Every believer has an inclination to set up a list of stipulations to follow. We all tend to rely on rules and regulations. We set up rules and put them on our mirrors in the bathroom or we put them over the sun visor in our automobile. One set may tell us how to relate to our children; another how to behave in an automobile. As legalistic, external stipulations, they do not work; however, they certainly do condemn us. The way the believer uses these stipulations depends on his understanding of what God is doing in bringing children into sonship. "The sting of death is sin; and the strength of sin is the law" (1 Cor. 15:56). The law strengthens sin. When we find a system of religion that relies upon a set of rules and regulations or behavior patterns as a basis for righteousness, it is carnal, cultic, and futile.

Source of Works

A set of rules prevents the believer, who becomes ensnared trying to keep them, to grow to sonship in

Jesus Christ. Sonship requires a believer to experience the new life from within. Then he will be able to maintain a consistent walk and understand the heart of God without external regulations. Remember, Paul said that the law was not written for the righteous man. Paul was not interested in sinning and no one had to keep him from doing wrong because he did not want to offend the heart of his Father. The pitfalls of sin still worked in his flesh, but his love for his Savior far outweighed the need to gratify those desires.

What God wants to build in the heart of the believer is an internal desire toward the will of God, a hunger after the Lord. The point is not to dwell on those times when righteous principles are violated. The point is the believer's sincere desire not to hurt the heart of God. When the believer goes against the advice of his conscience, a law will not help, for the choice has already been made. If he violated the rule, but did not want to, what benefit will a precept be? The believer violates righteous principles because the flesh is weak. Christ overcame the weakness of the flesh, both judicially and experientially, and He now lives in the believer. The indwelling life and power of Jesus Christ is better than any law.

"I have been [completed action in past time] crucified with Christ [with the present result that I am still crucified]; and it is no longer I who live, but Christ lives in me..." (Gal. 2:20 NAS). A law applied to the believer is a law applied to Jesus Christ because He now lives in us. Doesn't it seem more useful and even necessary to let Jesus live through us? The life that we now live is lived by the faithful Son of God, who is in us to will and to do His good pleasure (see Phil. 2:13). That is the liberty to which we have been born in Him.

Once we grasp this wonderful truth, we will understand that whatever is born of our labor for Him will be profitable for God. "...And the life which I now live in the flesh [remember, Paul distinguishes between 'me' and sin that operates in me—'it is no more I that do it, but sin that dwelleth in me' (Rom. 7:20)] I live by the faith of the Son of God, who loved me, and gave Himself for me" (Gal. 2:20). The next verse is so important. "I do not nullify the grace of God; for if righteousness comes through the Law, then Christ died needlessly" (Gal. 2:21 NAS). Jesus Christ had to come into the world as our substitute because we would never, under any circumstance or by any effort or means, be able to satisfy the righteous and just demands of an absolutely Holy God. If the law tells you not to go out and steal, you will not be righteous by obeying the law. "I do not nullify the grace of God." What do we do when we set up legalistic stipulations? We make void the grace of God. Since we are most certainly saved by His grace, then we would be voiding our salvation. Be careful that you do not limit this discussion of the law to the law of Moses. It applies to any law. "If righteousness comes through the Law [any law], then Christ died needlessly" (Gal. 2:21 NAS).

"And if by grace, then is it no more of works: otherwise grace is no more grace" (Rom. 11:6a). Paul said that grace and works cannot coexist in the work of God in redemption. God gives no ground on this matter. Either the forgiveness of God is free and unmerited or it is not given at all. An illustration from the Book of Genesis makes this point clear.

Adam and Eve's rebellion in the Garden resulted in a curse on the ground and a curse on the serpent. Man was not cursed, but the Lord cursed the ground for man's sake. God did rule on man's sin, however, and the judgment for man's sin was, "By the sweat of your face you shall eat bread" (Gen. 3:19). From the outset sweat has been associated with the fall and the judgment of God. When Cain brought his offering to the Lord, he offered what came out of the ground, which he got by the sweat of his face. Thus he presented to God the fruit of the curse. He had done nothing more than what God told him to do, earning his keep by the sweat of his brow. When he came to God, he merely presented his own obedience. God "had no regard" for his offering (see Gen. 4:5). Doing right does not represent man before God. On the other hand, Abel did not do what he was told. He tended sheep instead of tilling the soil by the sweat of his face. Thus, he brought before the Lord a substitute, the firstling of his flock. If we will take the text on the basis of what we are told, then Cain

was the good guy who did what he was told. Abel was
the one who chose another way, but Abel also was
the one who was accepted of the Lord because he
brought the substitute. Cain brought his own works.

When God gave the prophecy in Ezekiel concerning the restoration of the temple, He put a stipulation upon the priests who would minister in that
restored temple. He said, "They shall not gird themselves with any thing that causeth sweat" (Ezek.
44:18). It is obvious, if we feel we have to work at
something to please God, then God is not pleased.
The same principle can be found when God told
Moses the people were not to wear linen and wool together (see Deut. 22:11). You cannot mix the righteousness of God and the labor of man together.

If you and I are willing to rest in what God has already done and say, "Lord, I am as righteous right
now as I ever shall be or could be," then we become
satisfied knowing that God is satisfied. We can do
what He wants, not fearing the outcome, for if it all
goes wrong, we are togther with Him in peace. We
can never be more righteous than the blood of Christ
can make us. "For you have died and your life is hidden with Christ in God" (Col. 3:3 NAS). The importance of being dead in Christ is that it is the life of
Christ that is in us. If we will simply agree that we
died and that it is not we that do it anymore, but sin
that dwells in us, we would find release to enjoy being Christians. You instead may decide to "gut it out"

until the end. A lot of Christian experience is built on the statement, "I'm going to 'gut it out' until the end." Only then the end will come and you will have missed "life more abundantly."

Chapter 9

Futility of the Flesh

A witness is someone who reports what he has seen, heard, and experienced. A witness is not asked to take responsibility for or to render a decision. Decisions and verdicts are the judge's responsibility. John said, "...What we have heard, what we have seen with our eyes, what we beheld and our hands handled, concerning the Word of Life...we proclaim to you also, that you also may have fellowship with us..." (1 Jn. 1:1,3 NAS). We are to truthfully relate the facts according to our experience.

The *way* we declare the truth is another matter. A number of things may motivate our testimony to an individual. There are different types of motivation—some legitimate, some illegitimate. Fear of God is a type of motivating influence. On the other hand, valid ministry to an individual concerning the Spirit of God begins to quicken in the person listening the ability to receive truth. Often you can quickly sense if the hearer is receptive.

In the ministry of Paul, we observe that as he testified to the gospel, if the audience quit listening, then he quit talking. At one point he said, "You have judged yourselves unworthy of eternal life; I am going to the Gentiles" (see Acts 13:46). You may consider this an unchristian attitude, but Paul understood something that we often do not. We are not the savior. The message of the gospel is the power of God unto salvation (see Rom. 1:16). We are just the witnesses and nothing more. When a witness is called before a court of law, he is only allowed to describe what he saw and heard. The record then stands on its own merit. The Holy Spirit is the advocate for the Divine court and He helps our witness stand as the truth to the individual hearer. If He cannot make it truth, we never will. I am afraid we Christians have some misguided motivations. They may build a lot of churches, but they do not necessarily build the Body of Christ. When we begin to witness and find that we are being ignored, it is a good idea to stop. Paul said that while one sows and another waters, it is God who gives the increase. We do not have to "get a decision"; we must only communicate the truth. We are not taking scalps to be displayed before men. We are announcing the good news about Jesus Christ.

Very often we are privileged to be the witness who brings the repentant sinner to a saving knowledge of Jesus Christ. It is important he understand that, just as God has now received him through grace apart from works, his walk in Christ will also be through grace apart from works. Paul said that the Galatians had begun in the Spirit and then turned from the Spirit to attempt to come to maturity through the works of the flesh. All too often the new believer in Christ is, immediately upon conversion, given a new set of rules to follow. But a code of conduct only produces frustration, since he had already lost any hope of being righteous on his own. By offering him a set of rules, we have dealt him a deathblow and established the wrong basis for his walk in the future. Jesus was satisfied with "Go, and sin no more." In the walk of Jesus, He taught in principles and not in precepts. He presented principles that were in the precepts of the law. He brought out the spirit of the law rather than the letter of the law. Today we talk about the spirit and the letter with regard to our laws. Paul said, though, that the law was not given for the righteous man; he does not need it. It was given for the sinner, the adulterer, and the rebellious. A righteous man may break the law, but he does not break it intentionally. Therefore the law is of no help to him because he will keep it by desire and not by constraint. If he does violate the moral code, it will not be because of desire, but because of the weakness of the flesh.

The Letter of the Law

Jesus and His disciples were walking through a wheat field one Sabbath day and His disciples started to pluck the wheat and eat. When the Pharisees saw that, they said to Jesus, "See here, why are they doing what is not lawful on the Sabbath?" Jesus replied, "Have you never read what David did when he was in need and became hungry, he and his companions? How he entered into the house of God in the time of Abiathar, the High Priest, and ate the consecrated bread, which is not lawful for anyone to eat except the priests, and he gave it also to those who were with him?" (See Mark 2:23-28.) According to the law, it was not lawful for anyone to eat that bread except the priests. Jesus and the disciples were not Levites and only Levites could eat the showbread. But David and his men ate it and survived. David did not eat the bread because he was lazy and did not want to work; he and his men were hungry. There was a compelling reason.

Why was the law given with regard to the holy bread? The law was set down for the lawless. David was a man after God's own heart and God did not need to worry about David. What David did, he did with a view toward the glory of God. Never is the suggestion made that David was not a failure. On the contrary, God was very careful to publicize David's failure to let us know what kind of man he was. But David's heart after God dissolved anything he did wrong.

At the end of His confrontation with the Pharisees, Jesus said, "The sabbath was made for man, and not man for the sabbath" (Mk. 2:27). It is also true that we were not made for the Book; rather, the Book was made for us. This is difficult for some to understand because we have turned it around. In the New Testament, we have changed the Spirit into the letter.

I personally have experienced a classic example of this phenomenon. Some of the brethren of one city came to us saying they had a dilemma. They were dear brothers whom I had known for some years. They explained, "We have elders in our assembly. There is one man that we would like to add to that body. He shows all the qualifications of an elder. He has a real hunger for the Lord, and he is bringing forth fruit marvelously." They continued to praise the virtues of this man. So I asked, "What is the problem?" "He has been divorced," they replied. "After all, Paul said that an elder had to be the husband of one wife." This man had been divorced and remarried. So their question was, "What do we do?" I said, "Make him an elder."

The Spirit dissolves the letter. This man already met the qualifications. So why is that stipulation there? This stipulation is for the lawless man who wants to be a wife-trader. This potential elder had a bad experience in his life, and do we want to hold that over him when his heart is after God? What David did should have resulted in his being stoned, according to the law, but the fact that his heart was after God brought deliverance. Likewise, here was a man with a heart after God and he should have been an elder. The message of the Bible is to establish us in the faith, not to point out all our failures. This message is to produce the fruit of Christ in the lives of all who will hear and accept Him. Paul included this stipulation (e.g., Tit. 1:6) so the fellow who likes to trade wives cannot get into a place of authority. He does not belong in that place because he does not have a heart after God. If he cannot be faithful to one woman, then how could he be faithful to the Church of Jesus Christ?

I pointed out another of Paul's teachings to these brethren. In Romans 2 Paul speaks of the Jews who were proud of their place under the covenant of Abraham. Paul revealed their error. He said, "For when Gentiles who do not have the Law do instinctively the things of the Law, these, not having the Law, are a law to themselves" (Rom. 2:14 NAS). The idea is that, by observing the law, they establish the righteousness of the law even though they had not been given the law. His charge to these Jews was, "You Jews have the law, but you do not keep it." As a result the Gentiles who keep the moral standard of the law, in principle, become circumcised. On the other hand the Jews who have the law but do not keep it, in principle, become uncircumcised. Everything right about the Jews on the outside was made wrong because they did not have a heart after God. By the same principle, all that was wrong about the Gentiles was made right because they had a heart after God. The one thing God is after in His people is for them to hunger and thirst after Him. This brings

God's people into a right relationship with Him. Nothing else is necessary. The New Testament is void of any system of rules or regulations that apply to our walk in the Spirit.

The Hearing of Faith

If Paul had set down a set of rules, we could establish our righteousness based on whether or not we subscribed to them. We also would be putting them on everyone else. Yet in our heart we know that we would fail to keep those regulations. Therefore, we would come under condemnation at the very moment we were trying to impress other people of our godliness. That is exactly what the Pharisees did. They wanted everyone to consider them as the people of God, but Jesus said, "Do what they say, but do not do as they do" (see Mt. 23:1-3).

This is the only thing I want to find out from you: did you receive the Spirit by the works of the Law, or by hearing with faith? ... Does He then, who provides you with the Spirit and works miracles among you, do it by the works of the Law, or by hearing with faith? (Galatians 3:2,5 NAS)

So faith comes from hearing, and hearing by the word of Christ (Romans 10:17 NAS).

Too often we quote this verse from Romans as, "Faith comes by the Word of God." That is not what Paul says. Faith comes by the heart. Hearing comes by the Word of God.

At the pool of Bethesda Jesus walked up to the lame man and said, "Do you wish to get well?" The man replied, "I have no man to put me in the pool." Jesus said, "Arise, take up your pallet, and walk" (see Jn. 5:6-8 NAS). What was the lame man hearing? He was hearing the Word of God. When the Word of God comes, it creates the ability to hear God. When I can hear God, faith comes and I can walk in the ways of the Lord.

The Bible is the Word of God, but all of the words that God has spoken are not recorded in the Bible. It is imperative to keep in mind that any word from God will be consistent with the message of the Bible. I live in Texas because of the word of God, but no place in the written Word do I read, "Keith, go to Texas." God told me, out of my own mouth while I was preaching to another congregation, that I would minister in Comfort, using those exact words. So I ended up in Comfort, Texas. This was the God's word for me, but it was not in the Bible.

The word *scripture* is the Greek word for "writing" (*graphe*). It is usually referred to as the "Holy Writing." The Greek word *logos* means "word" and is the expression of the nature of God. There has been a great deal of attention given to the distinction between the words *rhema* and *logos*. *Logos* is the expression of the nature of God, but *rhema* is the spoken word of God. This is made clear in that verse from Romans, "Faith comes from hearing." Faith does not come by the *logos*, faith comes when we

170

hear the *rhema*, the word of God which is spoken or articulated. So when I hear the articulated word, it creates an ability to hear and thereby, believe God. The "hearing of faith" is that sensitivity of being able to obey the voice of the Spirit.

Chapter 10

A Heart After God

As I noted previously, there is a parallel between Galatians 3 and Hebrews 6. The approach is a bit different between the two books, but the principle is the same. It addresses the need to find rest in the finished work of Christ, and then walk in the maturity that the cross and the resurrection have given to us. We miss the meaning if we assume such phrases as "fallen from grace" and "crucify the Son of God afresh" refer to one's justification in Christ. These phrases, in context, only refer to believers who have a heart for God, but who only know him in a legalistic relationship. Therefore, they are walking by the flesh and not by the Spirit.

Let me remind you that the word *flesh* does not mean sin. Flesh will lead you to sin because the deeds of the flesh are sinful. Paul and Jesus tell us that the flesh is weak, so flesh simply means weakness. Paul also tells us that the law was weak through the flesh (see Rom. 8:3). The Book of Hebrews tells us that the law was a "carnal commandment," or a fleshly commandment (see Heb. 7:16). It was weak because we were caught in the system of the flesh (law) and, since we are flesh, the combination could only produce failure. The question in Galatians and Hebrews is whether we will come into a walk in the life of Jesus Christ through the flesh or through the Spirit.

Entering His Rest

Why is it important to enter into His rest in this present life? In the first place, we do not even begin to grow until we have entered into His rest. In the meantime, we go around in circles. We first travel to the wilderness of Zin (see Num. 13:21), then we go to the wilderness of Ziph (see 1 Sam. 23:14), and then to the wilderness of sin. Ultimately, we return to the place we started. All this circular course of activity is so we can gain knowledge and understanding of the Lord. As we learn, we discover the flesh is incapable of pleasing God and that our dependence must, of necessity, be totally on Him.

With this understanding, we are in a position to enter into the promised land, which is a symbol of His rest. This is what God did for Israel. It took them 40 years to learn the lesson. The lesson was, "In me (that is, in my flesh,) dwelleth no good thing" (Rom. 7:18a). God wants us to learn this lesson too, but we need to respond more quickly than Israel did. Even when we accept the truth, we find ourselves repeating the course on a regular basis. What is the problem? There is a great deal of difference between what our understanding appropriates and what our intellect appropriates. That is why God says, "...get wisdom: and with all thy getting get understanding" (Prov. 4:7). First God ministers knowledge to us, then wisdom, then understanding. Once we understand the object of the lesson, we begin to recognize God's plan and His way of using us. We begin to hear more than His words and His way becomes clear. The Galatian and Hebrew believers did not understand God's ways. They did not understand themselves; they assumed that God required some kind of cooperation from them in the great work He accomplished in redemption. What they failed to realize was their involvement only produced confusion.

Rebuilding the Legal System

But if, while seeking to be justified in Christ, we ourselves have also been found sinners, is Christ then a minister of sin? May it never be! For if I rebuild what I have once destroyed, I prove myself to be a transgressor (Galatians 2:17-18 NAS).

We have been delivered from the position of transgressor. "...God was in Christ reconciling the world to Himself, not counting their trespasses against them..." (2 Cor. 5:19 NAS). God, through Christ, has delivered us from our trespasses. If we set up the legalistic system again, we simply magnify our transgressions. Through the law, we set up a system that reveals what we were without the indwelling Christ. God has made a distinction between what we were and what we are now in Christ. That distinction is difficult for us to grasp. The phrase "old man" is used because it refers to something we were. The word translated "old," particularly as Paul uses it in Romans 6, is old as related to usefulness. It has nothing to do with age. The "old man" is old because he is no longer useful. He can no longer do anything for us. He has been crucified in Christ.

The New Man

The new man (in Romans 7:22 and Ephesians 3:16 Paul uses the Greek word for "inner man") is created in righteousness and true holiness. That is what God sees when He looks at the new man. Thus Paul is able to say, "But if I am doing the very thing I do not wish, I am no longer the one doing it, but sin which dwells in me" (Rom. 7:20 NAS). Sin was destroyed at the cross. That is the thing that is very difficult for us to get settled in our thinking.

Does this give license to sin? Paul says, "...How shall we, that are dead to sin, live any longer therein?" (Rom. 6:2) It is as natural for a redeemed man to want to do righteously as it was for him, before redemption, to do unrighteously. What we want to do comes out of our spirit and is pleasing to God, but what we feel like doing comes out of our flesh and cannot please God. I remember a pastor saying to me some years ago, "I am having a very difficult time getting my lost church members to live like Christians." Now not always, but quite often, the one who is taking license is one "having not the Spirit" (Jude 19). While the appetites of the flesh (body) would drive one to embrace sin, the appetites of the spirit would call one to righteousness. According to Paul, someone had made the accusation that he was preaching, "Let us sin that grace might abound." Paul's reply was, "Their condemnation [of such a message] is just" (see Rom. 3:8 NAS). The message of the grace of God is of such magnificent character that those who are not concerned with hungering after the Lord may well indeed see Paul's message as a license to be irresponsible. Such a license serves the purpose of revealing their hearts, does it not? I have yet to find a believer who is concerned about the deeds of the old man with a desire to pursue sin. The reason he searches out the difference between the old man and the new man—the flesh and the spirit—is that he wants to walk in righteousness and is trying to discover how to go about that. Those who stand back and say, "Well, there is a license to sin," do not hunger after righteousness. They have no motivation to pursue a close relationship with God. In the words of the poet of God, "Because they have no changes, therefore they fear not God" (Ps. 55:19).

We all understand that the believer will fail. He must, however, know that he is forgiven and any effort on his part to "do good" to restore God's favor is to no avail (see Gal. 3:1). "They crucify to themselves the Son of God afresh, and put Him to an open shame" (Heb. 6:6b). It looks to a second crucifixion of the Lord Jesus. To require a second crucifixion is to deny the finished work of Jesus. It is not necessary to crucify Christ the second time. Nothing more is required but to speak to Him. We can come boldly if we have a need only because we recognize that our access is by the blood. Let's settle this issue: *We will never be any more righteous than the blood of Christ can make us!* That is the only way of peace to the believer.

Obedient Hearing

Paul asks this question: "This is the only thing I want to find out from you: did you receive the Spirit by the works of the Law, or by hearing with faith?" (Gal. 3:2 NAS) Some translations use "the obedience of faith," but it is the Greek word "to hear." The same expression about faith is used in verse 5: "Does He then, who provides you with the Spirit and works miracles among you, do it by the works of the Law, or by hearing with faith?" (NAS) You will remember that earlier we differentiated between *logos* and *rhema* and found that *rhema* is the word used in Romans 10:17.

The issue of hearing is important enough to consider further here. In the Epistle to the Romans, particularly in chapter 5, the distinction is made between obedience and disobedience. The Greek word for obedience comes from two words meaning "to hear under"; the Greek word for "disobedience" comes from two Greek words meaning "to hear alongside of." Thus "to obey" means "to hear under."

In talking about Christ in His ministry in Romans 5, Paul says that men were made righteous in the Lord Jesus by one act of obedience (or by "hearing under"). In the case of Adam, it was his act of disobedience or "hearing alongside of" that caused all of man to be condemned. God spoke to Adam in the Garden and told him that of the tree of the knowledge of good and evil which was in the midst of the Garden, "...you shall not eat, for in the day that you eat from it you shall surely die" (Gen. 2:17 NAS). When Adam heard God, he believed what He said. Adam did not have any problem with it. He heard "under." The idea is to come under the authority of or to come under an obedience to someone. To come under God's word is to be submitted to that word. Adam came under it like we do an umbrella. But then another voice came in the Garden. The voice to obey comes down and the voice to be wary of comes alongside. So alongside the former voice came a new voice.

One tactic of the enemy is to imitate the voice of the Holy Spirit. For example, the enemy does not initially come to a believer and tell him to go out and commit a sin. The believer knows exactly where that encouragement comes from because there is no subtlety in that kind of urging. It is the subtlety of the enemy that we must be conscious of and avoid. What happened to the Galatian believers? They had been bewitched or beguiled. They had been subtly beguiled to listen to another voice. Did the other voice say, "Go sin"? No. It said, "Go, obey the law." Since the "strength of sin is the law" (1 Cor. 15:56), the deceiver, satan, says, "Go, obey the law." He tells you to do a good thing, but the good thing will kill you. The snake is subtle and imitates God's voice in suggesting a right thing, but to the wrong person or in the wrong way.

The burden placed on a well-meaning saint is often difficult or impossible to bear. The spirit indeed is willing, but the weakness of the flesh becomes ever so apparent even in an honest effort. The flesh itself is not sin, but because the flesh cannot perform, it produces the "works of the flesh," which come short of the glory of God. So what the law could not do in that it was weak through the flesh God sent His own Son to accomplish (see Rom. 8:3). Thus Jesus came, not made after the law of flesh (a fleshly commandment), but He came in the power of an endless life. Now we live, not under the weakness of a law that could not make us mature in our walk, but in the power of the Spirit of the life of Jesus Christ.

Legalistic systems cannot help the believer who has a heart for the Lord. They can only hinder him. If you know a man who wants to walk in righteousness, telling him what not to do is totally unnecessary. As a matter of fact, it may only make the situation worse because it aggravates his faults. It does not heal any of them. "Through the Law comes the knowledge of sin" (Rom. 3:20b NAS). To paraphrase Paul's words, "I was fine until the law came along and said, 'Thou shalt not covet.' " Then he said, "I died." (See Romans 7:7.)

Jesus, in speaking to the rich young ruler, recited the last six commandments. These concern our relationship to men. The first four dealt with our relationship to God. Jesus enumerated the last six because our relationship to God is revealed in our relationship with men. What did the rich young ruler say? "All these things I have kept; what am I still lacking?" (Mt. 19:20 NAS) The word *kept* means "to hold dear." In the marriage ceremony, the phrase "to keep only unto her so long as you both shall live" means "to hold dear." This young ruler had kept them or he had held the law dear from his youth. Paul had a similar testimony when he said, "As to the righteousness which is in the Law, found blameless" (Phil. 3:6b NAS). Paul had a heart toward God, but the law destroyed him because it condemned him for his failures and could do nothing to correct them. "Knowing this, that the law is not made for a righteous man, but for the lawless..." (1 Tim. 1:9).

The law was given as a sign and testimony to the nation of Israel and to declare the guilt of the world. It is the revelation of the knowledge of God, although very limited in its present form. When God added the law, He gave it to a people who had ceased to hunger after Him. Paul said, "For until the law sin was in the world: but sin is not imputed when there is no law" (Rom. 5:13). God would, by the law, hold man accountable for his actions. He would make sin to be sin. When Israel received the law, the people said, "All that the Lord hath said will we do, and be obedient!" (Ex. 24:7) What did Moses reply? "Behold the blood of the covenant" (Ex. 24:8). In other words, "You had better look well to the blood, for you are going to need it." When they set out to obey the law, they came to realize that they did not have the heart to obey. Abraham had a heart to obey God, yet Abraham had no law. Abraham became the friend of God with no rules to follow. Abraham enjoyed a relationship with the Lord, and still awaited the promise. "And all these, having gained approval through their faith, did not receive what was promised" (Heb. 11:39 NAS). We have received that promise, the promise of the indwelling Holy Spirit (see Gal. 4:1-7).

The Sabbath was a required day of rest for Israel and one they have not failed to observe. The Sabbath of the law was a foreshadowing of the perfect rest that was to come in Christ. That Sabbath finds its fulfillment in the finished work of Jesus Christ and those who believe (not work) they have entered into His sabbatical rest. Romans 4:5 and Hebrews 4:9-10 both address this rest that has become ours through the advent of the Holy Spirit into our hearts. "There remains therefore a Sabbath rest for the people of God" (Heb. 4:9 NAS). That rest is realized when we cease from our own efforts to be righteous and rest in the righteousness that is already ours through the finished work of Christ. We do not stop doing right things, but we do stop doing them for the wrong reasons.

The law was a shadow of things to come. You can buy a new car and sit down in the shadow of it and admire it, but it never does you any good as long as you sit in its shadow. You must get in the car and drive before it becomes useful. God has, in Christ, fulfilled all that the law foreshadowed. "And the Scripture, foreseeing that God would justify the Gentiles by faith, preached the gospel beforehand to Abraham, saying, 'All the nations shall be blessed in you' " (Gal. 3:8 NAS). We know they had a view toward the birth of Christ, but what does the word *gospel* mean? It means the "good news." The good news was preached to Abraham. What was this good news? It is that God would provide a satisfaction for sin apart from man's contribution. Galatians 3:12 (NAS) reads, "the Law is not of faith." No law is of faith, regardless of its origin. The verse continues, "on the contrary, 'He who practices them shall live by them.' " If we are under the law, or a law, as a standard of behavior, then we will reap the level of benefits that the law can provide. "For the law made nothing perfect..." (Heb. 7:19).

The fulfillment of the gospel preached to Abraham was the outpouring of the Spirit. The promise was realized on the Day of Pentecost and changed those who were justified to those who were saved. The difference between their being justified and their being saved was the gift of the Holy Spirit. Their belief caused them to be justified. The Spirit came so those who believed would be saved. It is by identifying with the cross and His resurrection that we are no longer children, but sons of God. Paul builds his letter to the Galatians around what is now available to us through the outpouring of the Holy Spirit. The "monkey wrench" in the works was that the Galatians were attempting to come to maturity by holding on to the works of the law. The law was instituted in Exodus 20, but for what purpose? To make us sons? Paul said, "No." The law was not given to make us sons. The law was given as a schoolmaster until Christ (see Gal. 3:24).

There are six words that we tend to fit together any way that seems convenient. The first three words are *flesh*, *law*, and *works*. The next three are *Spirit*, *faith*, and *grace*. If we want to draw a contrast to law, which word do we usually use? Grace. But that is not correct. God does not contrast law and grace. God contrasts grace and works. He contrasts law and faith, or promise; and flesh with spirit. God is consistent in these associations. Again, they are:

- flesh   vs.   Spirit
- law   vs.   faith (or promise)
- works   vs.   grace

When God refers to flesh and speaks of the counterpart, He talks about the Spirit. When He refers to the law and speaks about its counterpart, He talks about faith or promise. Together they refer to embracing what God has promised. Promise is what comes from God and faith is our response to that promise. Finally, if He talks about works, He contrasts it with grace. Thus Paul says in Romans 11:6, "But if it is by grace, it is no longer on the basis of works, otherwise grace is no longer grace" (NAS). He does this because "flesh" is a method of performance. "The spirit indeed is willing, but the flesh is weak" (Mt. 26:41b). This medium of performance, the flesh, is weak. It cannot do as it should. If we follow after the flesh, we cannot fulfill righteousness. In the flesh, we are totally dependent on our own ability to perform. If we follow after the Spirit, He performs for us. "For the law of the Spirit of life in Christ Jesus hath made me free from the law of sin and death" (Rom. 8:2). Flesh precipitates sin and death. The Spirit precipitates life and righteousness. If we have it by law, then it is dependent on the flesh to perform, and death is what comes. All the works of the law are vain (dead) works. But if we operate by faith, so receive it by grace and we produce the fruit of the Spirit.

Chapter 11

The Walk of Faith

Much has been written about faith and its importance in the life of the believer. What faith is and how it works is important to a walk of life that honors our Father. Although faith is not our savior (only Jesus Christ bears that title), it is by faith that we accept the saving grace Jesus brings to us. In essence, faith is our confidence in the truth of what He has promised.

Faith does not look at circumstances, at what is wrong with us or at how problems occur. Faith does not dwell on things as they "are," but rather on the things that "are not." "...The things which are seen are temporal; but the things which are not seen are eternal" (2 Cor. 4:18). If we continually focus on what is wrong with us, we will slip back under the flesh and be slain by the law. Paul said, "For if righteousness comes through the Law, then Christ died needlessly" (Gal. 2:21b NAS). Law and faith are incompatible.

How did God illustrate this to the children of Israel? He told them that they were not to sow two kinds of seed, such as wheat and oats, in the same field. Sowing them together made the field unclean. (See Leviticus 19:19.) This reminds the believer, who is "good ground," to be careful what he allows others to plant in his hearing.

There was nothing wrong with the law while the system of law was in effect. There is nothing wrong with walking by faith alone now that the age of grace is in effect. The point is to keep the law and faith separate so they do not get planted and take root together in the same "good ground." Paul says that the law was not given for the righteous man (see 1 Tim. 1:9), and we are now living in the age of righteous men who walk by faith. You will never be any more righteous than the blood of Christ can make you. This is the immutable position of the child of God in Christ Jesus. God has decreed us righteous and His Spirit now dwells within us. God is satisfied and He wants us to accept His satisfaction and not add to it. Of course, we do many things wrong. When we focus on the wrongs, though, we are no longer walking by faith, but by sight. Paul said, "I am no longer the one doing it, but sin which dwells in me" (Rom. 7:20b NAS).

We must turn our attention first to what God has accomplished. This is what Abraham did and he was no more without fault than you or me. The difference was Abraham believed God and his belief was counted to him for righteousness (see Rom. 4:3). Because

Abraham believed God, he followed after the Lord and God trusted him. This did not prevent Abraham from doing wrong. God was careful to tell us about the failures of Abraham. But since he had a heart to follow God, the Spirit dissolved his failures. The law could not have helped Abraham.

Abraham's faith was focused on the Seed that was to come. God said, " '...count the stars, if you are able to count them. ...So shall your descendants be.' Then he believed in the Lord; and He reckoned it to him as righteousness" .(Gen. 15:5-6 NAS). Four hundred thirty years after Abraham, the law was given because of transgression. It came to reveal wickedness and to slow the spread of evil. With the advent of the law, the wicked knew that judgment was inevitable. Those who walked after the Lord did so without the law because they had a heart after God. Another reason the law was given was to illustrate the manner and purpose for which Christ would die. He would die to redeem us from the curse of the law and from the death we received through Adam. Death reigned from Adam to Moses, but Christ came to abolish death and to offer us His life and immorality.

Imputation—Him for Us

God delivers us from the imputed sin of Adam and from our violations of the righteousness of God in Christ. When Christ died on the tree, all that He died for is illustrated in the law. The five offerings in chapters 1 through 5 in Leviticus demonstrate the following:

1. He is our peace that is the peace offering.
2. He is our success for transgression or trespass.
3. He is our sacrifice for sin—original sin, in Adam.
4. He is the three sets of sweet-smelling savor of righteousness.
5. He is a non-sweet savor offering—the substitute for all failure.

Concerning the law, Jesus is everything God required and He fulfilled all that was prophesied. When the children of Israel carried on the works of the ceremonial law, they were only setting out an object lesson and an illustration of the manner and purpose in which Christ would die.

Paul's greatest desire is to see people established in the faith. If we know where we are in Christ and understand our relationship with Him, we become free to receive all that God has for us. If we have any doubts about the security of our position, we will not receive anything and fall short of the maturity He has planned for us. In our minds, we think we have to return to the law to obtain righteousness. But Paul says that if we pursue our own righteousness by the works of the law, then we become ignorant of the righteousness and grace of God. If we walk in law, we do not walk by faith. We cannot mix the two.

Does this mean we are not contributors? Yes, that is exactly what it means. God is not asking anything from you and me. If He had needed anything from us, He would have settled that at the cross. He would have said, "It is almost finished." Since He requires nothing more than the cross, He said, "It is finished." He did not ask anything of Abraham. He simply told him what He would do. He promised Abraham a son and Abraham believed God. From that point forward Abraham was righteous in God's eyes.

If we walk in faith, we are blessed along with faithful Abraham (see Gal. 3:14). We are born from above, walking by that same faith and receiving the promise which Abraham anticipated by faith. Through the death and the resurrection of Christ, the promised Seed, we too have died to all that we were and have been raised to all that He is. We are born again, not of corruptible seed, but of incorruptible seed, which is the Word of God (see 1 Pet. 1:23). We now are no longer children of the slave master, but sons of the living God. No longer are we led by weak desires, but by the power of faith through His grace. This is the salvation of God.

The Savior's gift to us is faith, grace, and the Holy Spirit. These three work together as one. Therefore, our response to Him must be, "By faith, Lord, You are satisfied. I see what is so wrong with me, but I know, by faith, that You are satisfied." We see what we are, but we also see what God is and that He is greater than us. Where sin abounds, grace does super-abound (see Rom. 5:20). Through faith God administers His grace. "Let us therefore draw near with confidence to the throne of grace, that we may receive mercy and may find grace to help in time of need" (Heb. 4:16 NAS). When we draw near, grace is embraced. We may say, "But it all went wrong!" This may be true, but God, through Jesus Christ, makes it right.

The great example of this grace is the case of David and Bathsheba. David's actions were wrong and his thoughts and deeds contradicted the revelation of God. King David planned and supported a murderous deed in every way. There is no good found in David's stealing Bathsheba, arranging for the death of her husband, and then lying about the whole incident. Death was the inevitable judgment. But God brings life from death and so the God of all grace stepped in and fixed it. How did He fix it? He chastened David, but He also forgave David. He forgave David before he asked Him. As evidence of His grace, when the time came to put the seed of David on the throne of Israel, God chose Solomon, the offspring of his relationship with Bathsheba. In time the Messiah would be born of this royal line. How contradictory this is to our way of thinking. What is the Lord teaching us by this? Where sin abounds, His grace abounds more. This is how the Kingdom of God works.

Faith and Living

Faith will cause us to walk uprightly before God. "However, the Law is not of faith; on the contrary, 'He who practices them shall live by them' " (Gal. 3:12 NAS). According to the law in Leviticus 18:5, if you want to live, you have to do the law. Life under the law, though, does not produce more than a meager existence. "Christ redeemed us from the curse of the Law, having become a curse for us—for it is written, 'Cursed is everyone who hangs on a tree' " (Gal. 3:13 NAS). Christ has set us free from the law and its curse and in our new freedom we can pursue the fullness of God's promises. Galatians 3:14 reads, "In order that in Christ Jesus the blessing of Abraham [which is the promise of the Spirit] might come to the Gentiles, so that we might receive the promise of the Spirit through faith" (NAS). Faith brought us into the justifying work of Christ and will ultimately, by grace and through the outpouring of the Holy Spirit, bring us to the salvation of God.

Works or Faith

Often, in the minds of some believers, the Book of James causes a problem. James seems to suggest a conflict existed between his concept of faith and the apostle Paul's concept. Paul tells us that justification is by faith plus nothing. James, however, appears to be contradicting this position. Actually, James does not emphasize justification before God, but rather justification before men. If we understand that Paul is concerned with our justification before God, while James is concerned with our justification before men, the conflict is resolved. In other words, if our faith is genuine, it will do things that are upright before God. If it is not genuine, then it will do nothing that is useful in the Kingdom. James says, "...show me your faith without the works, and I will show you my faith by my works" (Jas. 2:18 NAS). Works become the evidence of faith, but works cannot help us obtain faith. The outward expression of our faith in word and deed is evidence of the presence of faith in us.

In the Book of Romans, Paul says that the gospel has been committed to him to bring about the obedience of faith among all the Gentiles (see Rom. 1:5). Faith always obeys. If one does not obey God, he testifies to his lack of belief. When the children of Israel refused to enter the land of Canaan, they did not believe God. Therefore, they did not enter the land. Hebrews 3:19 tells us that they "could not enter in because of unbelief."

"For whosoever shall keep the whole law, and yet offend in one point, he is guilty of all" (Jas. 2:10). That is precisely what Paul said in Galatians 3:10: "For as many as are of the works of the Law are under a curse; for it is written, 'Cursed is everyone who does not abide by all things written in the book of the law, to perform them' " (NAS). If we set up the law as the criteria for righteousness, we are suggesting that Jesus has not finished the work. If He has not finished the work of righteousness, then neither has He finished the work of justice. That would mean we would reap the judgment that comes through the law. The penalty of the law would still stand. The penalty of the law for failing to keep the Sabbath day is death by stoning. If we are to be consistent, that must be the penalty for those who break the law. Fortunately, God has delivered us by the body of Christ on the tree from the curse of the law: "Christ hath redeemed us...being made a curse for us" (Gal. 3:13a).

The Two Covenants

I want you to see the distinction between the Old Covenant and the New Covenant, where the cross is the dividing line between the two. When Jesus yielded up His spirit, the Lord is careful to tell us that the veil of the temple was rent in two from top to the bottom (see Mt. 27:51). According to Hebrews 10, the veil was symbolic of His flesh. In the Old Testament, the covenant sacrifice required the priest to divide the animal from the tip of its nose to the tip of its tail. The bloody halves were placed on either side of those entering into the covenant (see Gen. 15; Jer. 34:18). As they passed between the parts, they entered into covenant with one another.

The veil of the temple was rent in two and we have passed through the veil (His flesh) (see Heb. 10:20). By passing between the veil which has been rent, we have entered into the New Covenant with Him. Jeremiah prophesied of the New Covenant (see Jer. 31), a covenant that does not come to us as a law from without, declaring what we must do, but as a response from within by the indwelling Holy Spirit who establishes what God requires. God is giving us a new heart, writing His law in our minds and imprinting it on the fleshly tables of the heart (see Jer. 31:33). In all of this, God is satisfied with what He sees within the believer.

We have entered into that New Covenant by the blood of Jesus. If we compare the two covenants, we discover:

- Under the Old Covenant man was justified.
- Under the New Covenant we are saved.
- Under the Old Covenant man anticipated what God would do.
- Under the New Covenant, we have realized what God has done.

All of those who were under the Old Covenant gained approval through their faith, but did not receive what was promised. God had provided something better for us, in order that apart from us they should not be made perfect (see Heb. 11:39-40). Perfection is on the side of the rent veil where the Holy One dwells. Perfection is not immediate and the believer begins with his flaws. But He who is perfect, the Christ, completed the work and has come to live in the justified believer.

Chapter 12

Sonship

In Galatians 3:6-7 we read, "Even so Abraham believed God, and it was reckoned to him as righteousness [or justification]. Therefore, be sure that it is those who are of faith who are the sons of Abraham" (NAS). Sons is the Greek word *huios*, which speaks to maturity rather than *teknon*, which simply means "child" or "offspring." It is important that we distinguish between the way these two words are used. God speaks to two distinctly different stages of Christian growth with these two words. In the New Covenant, the purpose of God is to change us from a child (*teknon*) to a son (*huios*).

Galatians 4:4-5 tells us, "...when the fulness of the time came, God sent forth His Son, born of a woman, born under the Law, in order that He might redeem those who were under the Law, that we might receive the adoption as sons" (NAS). We have received that adoption as "adult sons" through the gift of the Holy Spirit. By His indwelling, we have been placed as sons in the Body of Christ. There are responsibilities and privileges that go with being a son. A son is free to fail, but he is not free to be irresponsible. To illustrate a son's responsibility, Paul discusses a son's behavior in the Father's house.

Under the Old Covenant, believers did not enjoy the privilege of being called "sons of God." Moses rightly deserves recognition, but often we fail to see the level on which Moses found it necessary to live. Did Moses ever enter the promised land? No, he did not. Did Moses go to Heaven? Of course, he did. The whole view of getting into the land is not comparable to going to Heaven. We have already been brought into the land through the finished work of Christ.

Ephesians 6:11,14 urges us to stand firm where we are. Paul does not tell us to take any territory, but rather to stand on ground that the Lord has already taken for us. The land is already possessed. It is our land and we are placed in it. If the believer fails to recognize his position, he lives out his life as a child rather than as a son. He may be a son positionally, but practically he is still experiencing childhood.

Therefore, while we acknowledge the greatness of Moses and talk of the marvels God wrought by his hand, we should not lose sight of the fact that Moses was, in fact, a child and a servant in the house. He was not a son in the house. As a servant, any authority he had was delegated to him. Hebrews 3:5 tells us, "Now Moses was faithful in all His house as a servant, for a testimony of those things which were to be spoken later" (NAS). Moses was a servant, but Christ is the Son. In Galatians 3, when Paul refers to the Seed of Abraham, he uses the singular noun form. Jesus, the Seed, is the only begotten Son. Through God, we are made sons of God because we have been made one with and in Christ Jesus.

How can we enjoy that distinction when the Old Covenant believers did not enjoy such distinction? They seemed to enjoy a much more intimate relationship with the Lord than most of us do. I think of David in particular, since he was a foreshadow of things to come. Much of David's experience was unique compared to other Old Testament believers. Psalm 27 is a record of the heart of David. "One thing I have asked from the Lord, that I shall seek; that I may dwell in the house of the Lord all the days of my life, to behold the beauty of the Lord, and to meditate in His temple" (Ps. 27:4 NAS). That is quite a statement from one who could not enter the Most Holy Place where the Presence and the Glory of God dwelt. Anyone who could express such a desire must have had a sincere desire to know the Lord. David was an Old Testament example of a New Testament experience. He was the exception and not the norm.

"But now, after that ye have known God, or rather are known of [by, NAS] God, how turn ye again..." (Gal. 4:9). Walking under the law kept them from knowing the Lord. There is a great difference between being known of (by) God and knowing God. Being known of God is a position of justification whereby the believing sinner stands in righteousness in the presence of a Holy God. God knows those who are His. In writing to Timothy, Paul says, "Nevertheless, the firm foundation of God stands, having this seal, 'The Lord knows those who are His...' " (2 Tim. 2:19 NAS). After the believer comes into Christ, the Father desires the believer to know Him. Knowing Him is the realization of eternal life, which is more than simply getting into Heaven. It is experiencing the life for which we have been redeemed. We must make it our prerogative to draw near to the Lord in the intimacy God has prepared for those who love Him.

The relationship between Christ and the Church is similar to that between a wife and her husband or the head and the body. The uniqueness of our position as sons depends on our becoming intimate members of the family of God. We are not adopted and placed into just any home; rather, we are born into the family. As children, we are adopted into the position of judicial sonship. In our Western culture the word *adoption* means to go outside the family, locate a candidate to adopt, and bring that one into the family. In early Oriental society the process was different. They could adopt anyone who was born in their household. We are born into the family of God as children (or "babes") and we are adopted as sons. Adoption relates to our judicial privilege in the family of God to function with the authority of the Father. When we receive the Spirit of adoption, God delegates His authority to us. For that to be possible, though, we must first be born into the family.

Under the Old Covenant, no one experienced the new birth. New birth is a blessing unique to the New Covenant, which results when we are raised from the dead in Christ. The first new birth occurred on the Day of Pentecost and since that day all who come to the Father through the Son become family members. As a result of our new birth, we were brought into a new relationship one in which the Holy Spirit made us "sons of God."

Some believers think the phrase "new birth" carries the connotation of being forgiven, but new birth is not forgiveness. New birth is what we experience because we are *already* forgiven. Forgiveness depends on the blood, but the new birth depends on the gift of the Holy Spirit. Forgiveness was available through atonement in the Old Testament. However, they could not be born again under the Old Covenant because sin was covered, yet not removed. Under this covering, the people went into the presence of the Lord justified. In faith, they believed God and were justified from all things and were assured of a place before the Lord in righteousness. Because they believed God, it was counted to them for righteousness. But under the New Covenant the blood does not just cover sin. It is better blood. What the Father did under the Old Covenant in covering sin was good, but what we have under the New Covenant is "better" because it includes the *removal of sin.* Jesus is the "firstborn from the dead" because He bore "away our sin" through His death on the cross (Col. 1:18; 1 Jn. 3:5). Now He is the "firstborn among many brethren," (Rom. 8:29) because sin is done away and we are new creations in Him. Through Christ Jesus the Father is bringing many sons into glory.

Experiencing Sonship

We have entered the position of sons through the resurrection of Christ and the gift of the Holy Spirit. This position is the result of receiving the Spirit of adoption, as mentioned in Galatians 4. However, having a position and walking in the provision and benefits of that position are not always the same. We begin as a child and we are nurtured to "apprehend that for which we are apprehended" (see Phil. 3:12). It was God's desire from the beginning that we would be sons. Sons do not walk by rules but by principles. The rule for the child is, "Do not leave your toys on the stairs." The principle to the son is, "Do not do what will cause injury to another." As a son, you are expected to act in a mature fashion.

The law was added because of transgressions. The law was not meant to, nor was it able to deal with, sin. Law is created for the lawless. The man who walks with the Lord is not forced into right action by the law; neither can the law make him do wrong. "The strength of sin is the law" (1 Cor. 15:56). Therefore, if we put ourselves back under a legalistic strain or ritual, we admit that we do not have a heart after God. We abandon our position as a child of God and must be treated like a servant in the household. We must be told every little thing to do. That is the way we deal with our children. Hopefully, they come to the point of spiritual maturity where they know what is right without being told. A good definition of sonship, then, is this: A son responds to the will of the Father without being told to do so.

"Therefore the Law has become our tutor [or, child trainer] to lead us to Christ, that we might be justified by faith" (Gal. 3:24 NAS). The "child trainer" or "schoolmaster" is *paidagogos*. This is the one who had the responsibility to get the child to school safely and then through school without him getting into trouble. That is the purpose of the law. Before the Spirit came, we did not know the way the Father wanted us to act. So God gave us the law. The law was like a protective hand rail placed alongside so we would not fall. Rails are also put on the sides of an infant's bed to keep the child from falling. The law was a security blanket for us until sonship. Why do we continue to rely upon laws? We have used the "rails" for so long that we are afraid to be without them. We are afraid we might fall. We are trusting in ourselves and not in Him who called us into this sonship.

The Lord has brought us into a large place and there is plenty of room to make a mistake. We have room to fall and still have confidence that He will lift us up. I have a real fear of high places. I can look at a picture in a magazine of the view from the top of a high building and, suddenly, my heart is in my throat. I can easily walk a brick wall if the wall is only a foot off the ground, but the thought of walking the same wall 60 feet high is overwhelming. Why can I not walk it up there, if I can walk it down here? That is the difference between the child and the son. To the son the height is not the issue, only where he is headed. We look not at the things which are seen. We look away from all else to Jesus, who is the Author and Finisher of our faith (see Heb. 12:2).

Paul states in Galatians 6:14, "But God forbid that I should glory, save in the cross of our Lord Jesus Christ, by whom the world is crucified unto me, and I unto the world." Through the cross, we have been separated from the world and the world from us. We are "in heavenly places in Christ" (Eph. 1:3). To know this is to have the truth that brings us into that experience as sons of God. Peter's walk on the water went well until he took note of the hostile environment around him. That was his downfall. Still, the Lord did lift him up, did He not? There is the first great lesson in sonship. "Though he fall, he shall not be utterly cast down: for the Lord upholdeth him with His hand" (Ps. 37:24).

Liberty or License

From Paul's perspective, it is the Lord's desire that we recognize the position of liberty into which we have been brought and that we put our attention upon the One whose life is within us. We must stop concerning ourselves with the problems that surround us and look to the "face of the Lord" (Lam. 2:19). The more we put our attention on the problems, the more we are engulfed by them and tend to reproduce them. Liberty is not license. Liberty is the right to do whatever you want. Does that sound like license? License is doing what God does not want, but liberty is the son doing the will of the Father from the heart. The nature of a son is to do the will of a father. The things that Paul "wanted to do" were the will of the Father. The things that Paul "would not do" were those things that would grieve the heart of the Father. The true and mature son always wants to do the will of the Father.

We spend a great deal of time trying to determine if everything we do is exactly what God wants. Actually there are many things that God would let us do that He does not care about one way or another. We are so concerned that we are doing the right thing that we forsake the privileges that are ours in the freedom of the Spirit. Paul said, "Happy is he who does not condemn himself in what he approves" (Rom. 14:22b NAS). In other words, God will let us make the decision about many things. Often, in reply to our request, the Lord will say, "I do not care if you do it or not. If you want to, then do it. Enjoy being a believer." Do not be concerned that this will provide an occasion to sin. For the son of God, sin is the last thing the son wants to do.

"...and if in anything you have a different attitude, God will reveal that also to you" (Phil. 3:15
NAS). If you start getting out of line, God will tell
you and He will not have to club you with a baseball
bat to do so. He will speak to you as a father to his
son and say, "Son, do not do that." It is a lovely and
loving thing to live as a son. Whereas the law sets
down all the stipulations and kills us if we fail, the
grace of God motivates from within. We are motivated to move after the Lord. Thus, if we do fall, He
is in a position to pick us up and say, "That's okay,
son, all is well. Let's keep on going." The law slays us
and leaves us there, but the grace of God restores
us and sets us in the Way. It has been said, "The
law brought God out to men, but grace brings men
to God."

I am a son, not because of my obedience to the
law, but by application of my faith. The law is not of
faith. "For you are all sons of God through faith in
Christ Jesus. For all of you who were baptized into
Christ have clothed yourselves with Christ" (Gal.
3:26-27 NAS). This adage bears repeating: "God said
it, I believe it, and that settles it." The truth actually
is, "God said it, and that settles it." God gives me the
truth and says, "Here is the truth—now live in that
truth." If I do not believe it, that does not change the
facts. "...Let God be found true, though every man be
found a liar..." (Rom. 3:4 NAS). Faith only deter-
mines the degree I enjoy the rest and blessing that
are provided to me as a believer in Jesus Christ

through the Spirit of Adoption. Those who believe Him are assured of entering into His rest.

This fact should now be settled in your mind: God says that we have been crucified with Christ. It is no longer we who live; rather Christ lives in us. The life which we now live in the flesh we live by faith in the Son of God, who loved us and delivered Himself up for us (see Gal. 2:20).

Are we going to believe that Christ lives in us? How do we usually judge our belief? We judge it by the way we behave. So, we say, "I am not behaving like Christ; therefore, Christ is not living His life in me." What does that have to do with His living in me? Why did Christ come? His purpose was to be a success in the midst of our failure. We will fail, but it is Him in us and He will succeed in our failure. He will be our righteousness before the Father in spite of our sin.

Again, we can take a look at our example of David and Saul. David's sin with Bathsheba gave the enemies of God an occasion to blaspheme. Saul disobeyed God by failing to kill all but one of the Amalakites. Whose sin was greater? Certainly, we agree on David. But who kept the crown? David did, of course. What made the difference? David was the one who had a heart after God. Nathan, the prophet, confirms God's grief over David's sin. "Why have you despised the word of the Lord by doing evil in His sight?" (2 Sam. 12:9a NAS) Yet when the time came to choose a seed to sit on David's throne, which wife was chosen to bear the seed? It was the wife of the sin, Bathsheba. God, by His grace, can take a thing that goes altogether wrong and bring right out of it. Jesus Christ was sent to nullify, to destroy, to loose us from the works of the devil. This does not mean that we will not do wrong anymore. When we do sin, His grace much more abounds (see Rom 5:20). "For the law of the Spirit of life in Christ Jesus hath made me free from the law of sin and death" (Rom. 8:2).

License

Paul was confronted with the charge of giving license to sin. "What shall we say then? Are we to continue in sin that grace might increase?" (Rom. 6:1 NAS) Usually, people who are worried about sin are worried about someone else's sin. "I know God can look after me, but I am worried about that other fellow so I am going to put him under the law so that he will walk straight." Why not release him to the same Spirit that is in us? Maybe the Lord can look after him as well as He can you. Paul declares in Romans 14:4, "...the Lord is able to make him stand" (NAS). Release him to the Lord. He has died. You are not releasing him to himself. The "self" in him is dead. You are releasing him to the Lord and God is able to make him stand.

It is through the new man that we are motivated to righteousness. Paul tells us, "How shall we who died to sin still live in it?" (Rom. 6:2b NAS) We have a new motivation through the indwelling Spirit. That is not to say we will not fail. David was on the housetop looking over toward Bathsheba and considering her beauty. He had plenty of time to consider the seriousness of what was in his mind, but he did it anyway. He gave in to the motivation of the flesh. David could say with Paul, "But if I am doing the very thing I do not wish, I am no longer the one doing it, but sin which dwells in me" (Rom. 7:20 NAS). God has separated us from the sin that dwells within and He recovers us from the results of it.

Thus, the true character of a son is that he wants to do the will of his father. We have become the very seed of Abraham through Christ and are the sons and the friends of God and the Lord Jesus Christ. God sees us as sons over His house. He has made us sons and we have come into the privilege of speaking and doing with the authority of the Father.

God's authority in action is seen in the life of Joshua. He commanded the sun to stand still and it did (see Josh. 10:12-13). He did not have a three-day prayer meeting to find out what to do. Prayer is continual communion and fellowship with God. We do not pray only to find out what to do next; rather, we establish communion and relationship so we know the heart of the Father. Then we can experience, through the Christ in us, what ought to be done in any situation within the sphere of our responsibility. We have the witness of the Spirit to guide us. We feel what our Father feels. "Even so Abraham believed God, and it was reckoned to him as righteousness. Therefore, be sure that it is those who are of faith who are sons of Abraham" (Gal. 3:6-7 NAS). Our primary concern should be the choice before us: childhood or sonship. We came into this world as a child of promise; we are born again as children of God. Through that position we become sons because of the adoption of the Spirit. The Spirit is sent into our hearts, and we are adopted and put into the place of sonship. As sons, the right or the privilege of expanding the inheritance is released to us. We have the power to do right.

Inheritance

The inheritance is only given to us now in "earnest" (see Eph. 1:14). The earnest deposit is not a down payment; it is given as assurance that the promised transaction will be finalized. If it is not finalized, then the earnest is not returned. So the earnest is what God has given to us to prove that the full inheritance is coming. Who has the right to do business with the earnest? Only the son has the right.

This was a concern of Abraham's before Isaac was born. "And Abram said, Lord God, what wilt Thou give me, seeing I go childless, and the steward [heir] of my house is this Eliezer of Damascus?" (Gen. 15:2) In this culture, a man without a son could assign the right of sonship to the eldest servant son born in his house. If the man died without a blood son, that servant would receive the inheritance. If Abraham did not have a son, his servant, Eliezer, would be his heir. In the Book of Proverbs, Solomon says, "He that delicately bringeth up his servant from a child shall have him become his son at the length" (Prov. 29:21).

This is all a grand illustration of what we came from under the Old Covenant. We were servants under the law. With the New Covenant, we have adoption as sons. As Gentiles we were outside the covenant, alienated from the commonwealth of Israel (see Eph. 2:12). Now we possess the covenant of promise and have been made sons by adoption. When Abraham was lamenting before the Lord about not having a son, he was simply saying, "I am going to have to give my whole inheritance into the hands of Eliezer of Damascus, and he is a servant in my house." God had a solution to that. "...This man will not be your heir; but one who shall come forth from your own body, he shall be your heir" (Gen. 15:4 NAS). When Isaac was born, he became the recipient of the entire inheritance. Ishmael, his half-brother, was only a participant.

What is the inheritance that has been committed to us? The world! (See Romans 4:13.) Do we have it yet? No. We have the earnest. The earnest is the Person of the Holy Spirit, who is the guarantee of our future possession. By living in the Spirit, we learn to use our inheritance. We learn what it is to be a son. When we have grown into faithful sons, we will be ready to receive the whole. "You were faithful with a few things, I will put you in charge of many things" (Mt. 25:21 NAS). Unless we learn to use the few, we will never rule over the "many."

Faithfulness

"For it is just like a man about to go on a journey, who called his own slaves, and entrusted his possessions to them" (Mt. 25:14 NAS). Why did the man entrust his possessions to them? He wanted to see how the servants would behave. Their behavior would determine what he would surrender to them upon his return. He would find out who were the faithful men in his house.

Paul told Timothy, "And the things which you have heard from me...these entrust to faithful men..." (2 Tim. 2:2 NAS). How do we know they are faithful? Watch them. Try them. Commit a measure of responsibility to them to see how they function with that before committing the whole to them. Solomon said, "But the prudent man considers his steps" (Prov. 14:15b NAS). The man gives the servant a little to see if he will be faithful with a little before he surrenders more to him. The way we raise children is a good example. Would I give my son a high-powered rifle when he is only eight years old? I might give him an air rifle. When time has passed and I am satisfied that he is capable of using it correctly, then I will consider something of a more serious nature. Children learn when we commit smaller responsibilities to them. In turn, we learn how they might respond to greater responsibility.

Measure

"And to one he gave five talents, to another, two, and to another, one, each according to his own ability;

and he went on his journey" (Mt. 25:15 NAS). He did not give them something they could not handle. Whatever you have, you can handle. Recognize also that the responsibility committed to one man may not be exactly the same as what is committed to another. It in no way diminishes what is in store for him, if he is faithful. The reason for the difference is that God will not commit to us anything for which we are not suited. The various ministries given to members of the Body of Christ are referred to as ministry "in measure." There is the measure of grace and the measure of faith. The measure of grace refers to what is committed to one and the measure of faith has to do with the manner in which it is used. Scripture speaks to the measure of grace in Ephesians 4:7 and to the measure of faith in Romans 12:3. That is the motivation of the earnest of the Spirit as He guided us in learning the Father's will and the Father's ways.

I have a measure of grace in teaching. My measure of faith, however, governs what subjects and in what geographical areas I teach. All of this is rooted in the motivation of the Person of the Holy Spirit, who is the earnest of my inheritance.

Romans 12:6 deals with measure regarding the gift of prophecy. "And since we have gifts that differ according to the grace given to us, let each exercise them accordingly: if prophecy, according to the proportion of his faith" (NAS). So the man with the gift of prophecy ministers in the measure of grace, but only within the realm of the revelation given to him. For this reason it is damaging to compare ministries. We do not all have the same commission. Paul and Peter both had the same measure of grace; they were both apostles. They did not have, however, the same measure of faith. Paul's measure was to the Gentiles whereas Peter's was to the Jews (see Gal. 2). There is no diminishing of quality, only a difference in responsibility.

Do not bury your talent in the ground because you think it is not important enough or grand enough. The Lord of the house will come and say, "What have you done with what I have given you?" When we have to report that we gained nothing, then even that grace ministry which we have will be taken from us.

In the Garden, God gave Adam authority and dominion over the whole of His creation. What did He tell Adam would be his vocation? He was to be a natural scientist. "Fill the earth, and subdue it" (Gen. 1:28). That meant Adam was to make the earth work for him. God was telling Adam to expand the inheritance He had given him. Adam was to make things out of God's creation and to create things that will be an expression of his ability as God equipped him. The result would be to man's honor and to God's glory. Adam, however, committed a faith act to the devil and brought the whole of creation under the authority of satan. Thus there is a motivation within us to do what God told Adam to do. The problem is, we are trying to do it without God. In the words of the prophet Amos: "Thou shalt die in a polluted land" (Amos 7:17). That is true for us too because we are doing it without God. God gave Adam the privilege of being a laborer "for" God and he rebelled. Now, through the redemptive work of Christ Jesus, we have been made "labourers together *with* God" (1 Cor. 3:9). Our labors are preparation for the day when the redeemed of all the earth will be brought again to the Eden of God, that they might do what Adam failed to do. The redeemed are to expand the inheritance, to take the whole of God's creation and begin to make things out of it. If I am not wrong, it will be unlike any other vocation ever seen before. The degree of our responsibility will be dictated by how we deal with the measure of the earnest that is committed to us here and now. Let us therefore walk as sons and not as children.

Chapter 13

Motivation From Within

"My children, with whom I am again in labor until Christ is formed in you" (Gal. 4:19 NAS). "It was for freedom that Christ set us free; therefore keep standing firm and do not be subject again to a yoke of slavery" (Gal. 5:1 NAS). These two verses are directly related. Paul is dealing with sonship in this epistle. A son is one who has been placed judicially in a position to speak with the authority of and move with the mind of the Father.

The apostle Paul is careful to tell us that we have the mind of Christ (see 1 Cor. 2:16). He also exhorts us to "Let this mind be in you" (Phil. 2:5a). There are two different Greek words translated "mind" in these two epistles. In First Corinthians the idea deals with the vehicle or capacity to think as God thinks. In Philippians, Paul exhorts us to use that mind as it was intended. He wants us to "develop the attitude of Christ." Sonship then, by experience, is letting the nature of the renewed mind flow out. What we have been given in the new birth is the potential for a new value system and a totally new frame of reference.

The law came to us before from without and commanded flesh to perform in a spiritual way. Since it could not, the law brought us down in judgment and we died. Paul said, "And I was once alive apart from the Law; but when the commandment came, sin became alive, and I died" (Rom. 7:9 NAS). Therefore, God has now given us a new character and potential that have removed us from the flesh and servanthood and have brought us into the position of sons. This is another result of the new birth.

The new birth is not forgiveness. We are born again not to be forgiven, but because we are forgiven. We are forgiven through the blood and are born again by the power of the resurrection. Together the result is salvation. To understand the letter to the Galatians, the distinction has to be made between the believer in a justified position and the believer in a saved position. We tend to take the word *salvation* and tack it on anything and everything that concerns going to Heaven. Heaven is not the primary focus of salvation. Abraham went to Heaven, but he did not know the salvation of God. Noah went to Heaven, but he did not know the salvation of God. The salvation of God depends on *God's bringing His life into us, and the outflowing of that life by the indwelling Christ. That is what the new birth is all about.*

Indwelling Life

Jesus was raised from the dead by the power of the Father (see 1 Cor. 6:14). We are, in Him, raised from the dead by the power of the Father as well. The life that dwells in Him now dwells in us and that is what precipitates the salvation of God. The only way we can experience the practical outworking of God's salvation, though, is to surrender to that indwelling life rather than follow an external code.

Under the Old Covenant mankind did not have the indwelling life of Christ. If they were believers, God was with them, but not in them. If they were not believers, they still had the moral nature of God written on their hearts (conscience). There is a problem with the conscience, however. Man commands it, but it does not command man. The conscience can tell us whether something is right or wrong. If we reject the conscience to gratify our carnal desires, the next time we are faced with a choice, the conscience becomes less capable of discerning right from wrong. We go from a defiled conscience, to an evil conscience, to a seared conscience (see Tit. 1:15; Heb. 10:22; 1 Tim. 4:2). At that point, we no longer respond to the dictates of the moral nature of God that are written on the heart of every man, whether he is regenerated or not. But now, through the salvation of God, He can live and rule with a new power over the mind and conscience of every man who has been raised in new life.

Fullness Through Obedience

There are two expressions in Scripture with regard to the giving of the Person of the Holy Spirit. In Luke 11:13 the "heavenly Father give[s] the Holy Spirit to those who ask Him" (NAS). In Acts 5:32 is the "Holy Spirit, whom God hath given to them that obey Him." Both of these cases do not deal with redemption, but rather with the anointing and empowering of the Spirit of Christ in the believer.

In Ephesians 5:18 we have the fullness of the Spirit; in Ephesians 4:13 we have the fullness of Christ; and in Ephesians 3:19 we have the fullness of God. What a grand progression in the knowledge of Him. There is a lot of talk about the fullness of the Spirit, less about the fullness of Christ, and even less about the fullness of God. In the tabernacle of Moses in the wilderness, the Outer Court is the place of the fullness of the Spirit. This is open to all. The fullness of Christ is seen in the Holy Place, the place reserved for communion and revelation. The fullness of God can only be experienced in the Most Holy Place, the residence of His Glory, which is His Light. The psalmist said, "In Thy Light shall we see light" (Ps. 36:9b).

A great many Christians have been content with the fullness of the Spirit. People are motivated for the most part by their feelings. Since the filling of the Spirit can, and often does, affect our feelings, we are content to stop at this point. Unfortunately, those feelings are only a reaction of the body *to* that filling, but the believer is not full. These feelings can become an avenue of attack for satan. God always starts with the spirit of man and moves to the soul. Then the body is brought under His control. Satan, on the other hand, always starts with the body and moves from there to seduce the soul. If he can gain access through the body, he has a chance to control the soul of a man. Romans 6:16 tells us, "Do you not know that when you present yourselves to someone as slaves for obedience, you are slaves of the one whom you obey...?" (NAS) If we yield our members as instruments for unrighteousness unto sin, then satan takes a measure of authority over us because we have submitted to him and come under his authority.

For example, if I leave the United States and go to Mexico, I am still a citizen of the United States. However, I willingly submit myself to the laws of Mexico as long as I am in that country. If I break a law in Mexico, then I am subject to that law even though I am still a citizen of the United States. Likewise, if I submit myself to the word of satan and by that vex the Spirit of God, then I will have to suffer the consequences. I am chastened as a consequence. "For whatsoever a man soweth, that shall he also reap" (Gal. 6:7b). Of course, that crop itself is a vehicle of God whereby He teaches me the lesson of obedience. That fits neatly into the program of the chastening of the Lord. "And we know that God causes all things to work together for good to those who love God, to those who are called according to His purpose" (Rom. 8:28 NAS). This "all things" is not a qualified phrase. God wants to bring us from the fullness of the Spirit to the fullness of Christ, so He might ultimately bring us to the fullness of God. Our Father matures us from the less holy to the most holy.

The Body Builds Itself

Ephesians 4:16 (NAS) reads,

From whom the whole body, being fitted and held together by that which every joint supplies, according to the proper working of each individual part, causes the growth of the body for the building up of itself in love.

The "from whom" in this verse is Christ. Look at the phrase, "building up of itself." I think that is a remarkable phrase. The body is capable of edifying itself from within. Within each of us is the ability to contribute to the growth of the Body of Christ. Using what God supplies to each one of us, we can inject our portion into the Body and the whole Church grows until it comes to the fullness of the measure of the stature of Jesus Christ (see Eph. 4:13). The carnal commandment could never accomplish this. It required a new order and a new life.

The New Covenant has taken away our stony hearts and given us hearts of flesh. Hebrews 10:16 quotes Jeremiah: "This is the covenant that I will make with them after those days, saith the Lord, I will put My laws into their hearts, and in their minds will I write them." Now the law flows out from us rather than coming to us. The believer has the privilege of choosing his life style. We have the choice to live as children under the law or as sons under the grace of God.

There is a lesson to be learned from the story of the prodigal son in Luke 15. I think it is as much the story of the elder brother as the prodigal son. Even though the younger asked the father for his inheritance and squandered it, the elder did nothing with his. The elder said to his father, "You have never given me..." and the father answered, "All that I have is yours." What is the implication? The elder son never used what he had the authority to use. He never did anything bad with it, but at the same time, he never did anything good with it either. He did nothing with it. The prodigal did something, even though it was not good. He learned a costly, but vital lesson. The father got back an educated son. After the younger had gone that route, he learned something that the elder brother had not learned. When he returned, having invested in riotous living, he learned the results of irresponsible living. He went out a child, but when he returned, he received another portion of the inheritance, for he came back a son.

I am the Lord, and there is no other; besides Me there is no God. I will gird you, though you have not known Me; that men may know from the rising to the setting of the sun that there is no one besides Me. I am the Lord, and there is no other, the One forming light and creating darkness, causing well-being and creating calamity; I am the Lord who does all these (Isaiah 45:5-7 NAS).

Did God know man would fall when He put him in the Garden? Of course He did, but out of that experience, God gets many sons for glory. It would have been wonderful if the prodigal had acted like a son to begin with and avoided the misery he inflicted on his father and on himself. It would have been much better if he could have realized the blessing of being a son without having been taught the hard way. However, he learned the truth the only way he could. After completing the lesson, he came back to the father a son, a safe son, a trusted son. The elder brother had not learned anything. That is the message of the story.

Death Before Life

I suppose you would say, "Let us put some regulations on the son. Let us tell him, 'Now look, son, you do not leave home and go out and feed hogs. I am going to anchor you here, and I am going to show you the good and right way. I will do it with some laws.' " The father did not do it that way. You see, laws do not make a bad man righteous. They make him a transgressor. That is why the law was given. As we saw earlier, the law was given to make a person a transgressor. As transgressors, we were not expected to be righteous. It only made clear the grossness and the wickedness of our sin. Sin, by the law, would become exceedingly sinful. Once we realize our lack of character and wrongful behavior, God can institute a new principle. Before He does, though, we must die. By the new birth, then, we can have life with a capital "L." That is what the new birth is. It is resurrection from a former dead state *to* and *through* and *in* His Life.

Hebrews 7 illustrates that the way of the Lord Jesus is superior to the Old Covenant. He is better than Moses, better than Joshua, and better than Canaan. In this passage He is better than the Aaronic priesthood. "Who has become such not on the basis of a law of physical requirement, but according to the power of an indestructible life" (Heb. 7:16 NAS). Another word for "physical" is "fleshly." "Who has become such not on the basis of a law of *fleshly* requirement...." Since it is fleshly, it depends on the flesh to fulfill its requirements. The flesh "is not subject to the law of God, neither indeed can be" (Rom. 8:7). Again, we must remember that the flesh is not called sinful; it is called "weak." Because the flesh is weak, its works are sinful. It cannot perform because it is weak. So if the law is called "fleshly," is it then sinful? Of course not. It is weak through the flesh, and therefore cannot do the deeds of the law. Paul says, "For Christ is the end of the law for righteousness to everyone who believes" (Rom. 10:4 NAS).

Jesus and the Sabbath

Jesus was not made after the law of a carnal commandment. He was made under the law, but He exceeded the law. All that the law required was incorporated in Him because the Author of the law was incarnate, and demonstrated the righteous principle and character of that law.

The Pharisees who were committed to the law could not understand this. That was why they had such a hard time with Jesus' actions on the Sabbath day. Jesus healed a man with a withered arm on the Sabbath and they said, "Six days in the week men ought to come to be healed..." (see Lk. 13:14). The Pharisees missed it altogether. The Sabbath is indeed the rest of God. Our old labors and burdens are set aside and a new energy and new life become ours. We can walk in the sabbatical of the Lord. Jesus demonstrated it, but the Pharisees missed it. That is why Paul goes on to say, "But as at that time he who was born according to the flesh persecuted him who was born according to the Spirit, so it is now also" (Gal. 4:29 NAS).

Carnal or Spiritual?

Those who move under a carnal traditional system can never understand those who move under a spiritual traditional system. I use that word *traditional* advisedly. If we intend to walk under a carnal system, we will have the situation illustrated earlier—the "wilderness of woe"—wherein we need regulations to dictate how we are to behave.

Forgive me if I lay hands on a "golden calf," but this is why we set up church covenants—so everyone will know how to act. To use a simple illustration, I am not concerned about a Christian wanting to rob a bank. He will not have that desire. God has given us new desires. The new desires He placed within us are what turn us away from the old things that the law could tell us not to do, but gave us no energy to avoid. That is the grand result of the new birth. To paraphrase Paul, "I am worried about you, Galatians; I am concerned that I have bestowed labor on you in vain. You have missed the whole point. You are going back under these weak and beggarly elements that only bring you into bondage and can do nothing for you. They only satisfy the flesh." (See Galatians 4:9-11.)

Indwelling By Faith

You may have heard someone say, "I do not feel that God is in me." Obviously the Galatians did not either, but Paul was careful to point out in his Epistle to the Ephesians that Christ is to dwell in our hearts by faith (see Eph. 3:17). Christ dwells in the heart of the believer by faith and not because we feel Him. What we feel is totally immaterial. We may feel like the worst creature that ever crawled across the face of God's green earth. Still, how we feel is irrelevant because Christ dwells in our hearts by faith.

The Spirit of God is there to manifest His Son and the savour of His knowledge is revealed by us in every place—*period!* There is no stipulation in the Scripture that says we must feel God in order for Him to be in us and with us. Let the life of Jesus Christ, which is in you, flow out without your getting involved. The fruits of righteousness will flow by Jesus Christ (see Phil. 1:11).

Yielding

We often become ensnared after we have submitted to the Lord because we think it is up to us to fulfill His life. We say, "All right, Lord, I am going to yield to You. Now, let's see; what do I need to do now that I have yielded?" That is where we miss it. It is really difficult for us to do nothing. We are certain that it is incumbent upon us to do something. To the contrary: "For it is God who is at work in you, both to will and to work for His good pleasure" (Phil. 2:13 NAS).

There is no doubt that our Father desires a fruitful life from His people. The prerequisite of fruit, though, is to wait on Him. It is so important that I learn to "be" before I try to "do." That time of waiting is often frustrating and embarrassing to us. We think it does not "look" right to others. Yet Jesus never found it necessary to explain what He did or why He did it. He depended on the Person of the Holy Spirit to defend or to authenticate His deeds. Why can we not do the same? When we are willing to sit and do nothing for days on end, we will stop struggling to "perform."

That is why Mary's actions aggravated Martha. Those who live in the "doing mode" of the flesh will always persecute those who walk by the Spirit. That is why Martha says, "I am busy; why aren't you?" We can get busy in a hurry. We can think of all kinds of busy things to do, but what eternal value do they have? They may only serve to make us look good before others. When we come into His presence in that day, if our works are all burned up, it will be just "wasted sweat." God said to the priests of the Lord, "They shall not gird themselves with anything which makes them sweat" (Ezek. 44:18b NAS). Our first concern should be about who we are and that will take care of what we do.

Waiting on Him

The scriptural ideal for waiting on the Lord is to meet with Him in the early morning hours, before the din and confusion of the day comes down upon us. The psalmist said, "And in the morning shall my prayer prevent [precede] Thee" (Ps. 88:13b). We must watch our motive. There is a feeling that if we do not come early in the morning, we miss God the whole day. We must take care not to make a law out of it; otherwise we will condemn ourselves when we miss the time.

Suppose you get a call at four in the morning and you have to go out? When you return the day is filled with "things" and when you come home at the end of the day, you are completely fatigued. Before you know it, it is midnight. With one interruption after another, fatigue has become exhaustion. After falling into bed, the condemnation begins to come. "You did not wait on the Lord today." The next morning you are too tired to rise early. It is seven o'clock before those weary bones will get up. What is often the attitude at this point? "Today will be a bad day; I did not meet the Lord." This is a sad view of the God we serve. Does the river of God, which "is full of water," not suffice? Do those "living waters" that come out of us from His indwelling presence fail so quickly to flow?

The manna in the wilderness illustrates this point. They were to gather the "bread of heaven" each morning and it was good only for that day. (However, remember that what was gathered on the day before the Sabbath lasted through the Sabbath.) According to the Epistle to the Hebrews, we are now, through the finished work of the cross, in God's Sabbath day. "For he that is entered into His rest [sabbatical rest], he also hath ceased from his own works, as God did from His" (Heb. 4:10). It should be noted that the wilderness and the manna was only temporary. They pointed to a schoolmaster relationship. In the land of promise the manna would cease and they would eat of the old corn of the land. There was no time stipulation on eating the "old corn." Here was Christ in His fullness. Here was the bold entrance into the "throne of grace, that we may obtain mercy, and find grace to help in time of need" (Heb. 4:16). He is always there for us.

This is the attitude of communion that should exist between the believer and the Father. This is what Paul meant by praying without ceasing (see 1 Thess. 5:17). It is not praying all the time. No one can, or does, do that. Your mind cannot do two things at once. Paul did not pray while he was preaching, but he did not preach without praying.

To use a personal illustration, suppose my wife and I are going on a trip, just the two of us. When we rise in the morning I greet her not with long flowery phrases, but with a kiss and perhaps a cup of coffee. We chat a bit about the day ahead. Then, when the traveling needs are settled, we go to the car and depart. We may talk for an hour or so, but then perhaps say nothing for some time. We do not "sign out" by saying, "In your name, amen." We just cease conversation. Time passes and perhaps something will catch her attention. She does not "come back into my presence" with "Oh, thou august husband that provideth food for all my meals, who bringeth home the check, who seeth to it that my children are clothed and trained; hear me, oh thou august husband." Of course not. She simply speaks to me as if the conversation had not ended. "Look at that, honey, isn't that a beautiful home?" How simple that is.

Most of us tag "in Jesus' name" on the end of our prayers just so everyone will know we are through praying. How much of the terminology of our prayers is for the benefit of those who are listening rather than for the One to whom we speak? This is a subtle, subconscious thing. Our concentration is really not on the Lord, but on those who are around us. This is only a symptom indicating our lack of intimacy with Him.

We read earlier in Galatians,

But now that you have come to know God, or rather to be known by God, how is it that you turn back again to the weak and worthless elemental things, to which you desire to be enslaved all over again? (Galatians 4:9 NAS)

He can only be referring to a people who had a personal relationship with the Lord, but had regressed to a place where God simply knew them. They no longer knew God. Every believer is known by God, but not every believer knows God. I assume all Christians talk to the Lord periodically, but not every believer really knows the Lord to whom he talks. He simply talks to some abstract concept in the upper atmosphere. These believers feel a separation because He is up there and we are down here. Every now and then we go to Him and communicate with Him, laying all our needs out before Him. Then we leave Him and go off to do the best we can, hoping He will help. That is not the kind of relationship God chooses. We are the bride of the Son. We are with Him and He is in us in all circumstances. We are in a constant communion with Him. We have a continuing relationship and by that relationship we can "eat of the old corn of the land" at all times (Josh. 5:11). This is what keeps us in the way of righteousness—a continuing communion with Him.

It is also a continual flow of life. I am confident my wife will not willingly do anything that offends me. I know that because she loves me. "Love does no wrong to a neighbor" (Rom. 13:10 NAS), nor a wife to her husband. Because of my confidence, I have no need of suspicions. If she were to "fall," there would be no rejection of her, for love covers a multitude of "falls" (see 1 Pet. 4:8). Furthermore, it is my responsibility to "absorb" the wrong because "the husband...is the savior of the body [bone of his bone and flesh of his flesh]" (see Eph. 5:23).

To know that God loves us and to live in that love is not only to walk in peace, but also to have the assurance of His ever-present forgiveness. Love begets love and His love working in us will return a love to Him that makes us "safe sons." It is not the threat of His wrath that keeps us straight, but a desire not to hurt the One who so loves us and whom we love in return. How completely "undoing" it is to have our Father show us an act of love and kindness on the heels of one of our worst failures. It is "the kindness of God [that] leads you to repentance" (Rom. 2:4 NAS). As Zacharias, the father of John the Baptist, put it, this kind of knowledge allows us to "serve Him without fear" (Lk. 1:74).

Chapter 14

The Cross Plus Nothing

The first three chapters of Galatians establish what God has done for us through the gift of the Holy Spirit and His relationship to our position as sons who have been delivered from the law. The fourth chapter deals with that position as sons in the Body of Christ. If we are sons, what should be evident from that position? The law demanded obedience, but we could not perform it. Now love brings a spontaneous response of obedience to the Man Christ Jesus that the law could never accomplish.

Stand Fast

The message in Galatians 4 is, "stand fast in your liberty." God has brought us into a position as sons, so we should stand in freedom as sons and not as children under regulations. We should walk as adults who know what needs to be done. We then do it because it is the right thing. We are moved by our relationship with the Father and not because it is required of us as servants. "Stand fast therefore in the liberty wherewith Christ hath made us free, and be not entangled again with the yoke of bondage" (Gal. 5:1).

Galatians 5 is a warning and an exhortation. It is similar to Hebrews 6. Justification is by faith through grace alone (see Eph. 2:8). If one is to bear the fruit of the Spirit, it must be by faith through grace alone. Paul warns that to receive circumcision as an avenue to justification is to reject the grace of God and the cross of Christ. Obligating oneself to any part of the law makes one a debtor to the whole law (see Gal. 5:3).

Some argue that Christ only did away with the ceremonial law, that when Paul addresses circumcision he does not include the Ten Commandments. Two passages point out and assure us that he had the whole law in mind.

In Colossians 2 Paul warns the believer that he is not to allow himself to be judged by the legalizer with regard to holy days or even of Sabbath days (verse 16). This releases the Christian from the requirement of the fourth commandment. Then in Romans 7 in his discourse on the bondage and death that the law brings, Paul refers to the tenth commandment, "thou shalt not covet," as the one that slew him (verse 7). In effect, through this one commandment God said, "thou shalt not *want* to do any of the 'shalt nots.' "

Paul's reference to these two commandments make it plain that when he refers to the law, he refers to not only the ceremonial law but also to the moral law. One might keep the ceremonial law. It was the moral law, the commandments, that slew. So as Paul tells us in Romans 11, if it is works, then it cannot be grace. If it is grace, then it cannot be works. (See Romans 11:6.)

The conclusion, then, is this: Any sort of regulation, whether from Moses or from another, that is placed upon the believer with a view toward *obtaining* right standing with God or *maintaining* right standing with God, is legalism and results in death. So when Paul speaks to circumcision, he is encompassing the whole of the law. "And I testify again to every man who receives circumcision, that he is under obligation to keep the whole Law" (Gal. 5:3 NAS).

James reenforces this in James 2:10. "For whoever keeps the whole law and yet stumbles in one point, he has become guilty of all" (NAS). In other words, with the law it is perfection or nothing. "For as many as are of the works of the law are under a curse; for it is written, 'Cursed is everyone who does not abide by all things written in the book of the law, to perform them'" (Gal. 3:10 NAS). Since the Old Covenant brought guilt, God provided the believer with a "mercy seat" for his failure. Under the New Covenant, God brings life and provides the believer with access to His "throne of grace." The believer is invited to come "boldly" for help in time of need. (See Hebrews 4:16.)

The Message of Life

The message of life in the New Covenant is that love performs through me what the law outside of me could not. Suppose a preacher says, "You must love God." Has he told you the truth? No. He has told you something that is true, but there is a big difference between what is true and what is the truth. It is true because God said it. It becomes the truth when it is used the way God uses it. If I tell you that you must love God, I have not ministered life to you as good news; I have ministered bad news and death. We cannot love God. We love darkness. We do not have the machinery to love God. What is the answer? We must confess our inability. "Lord, I do not love You." What does God do? He says, "But, I love you anyhow." The truth is that even though I should love God, I do not and cannot love God. To His honor and glory, He loves me anyhow. Now I begin to learn that love begets love. "We love Him, because He first loved us" (1 Jn. 4:19). The beginning of an abundant life with God is to know that God loves you. "Herein is love, not that we loved God, but that He loved us..." (1 Jn. 4:10). Knowing, receiving, and experiencing His love creates love in me for Him, for His Church, and for those in need around me.

I find it interesting that Jesus was far more interested in what a man *wanted* to do than He was in what a man *did*. Romans 7 is a testimony to what Paul wanted to do. He, with his mind, served the law of God, but with the flesh he served the law of sin.

God saw what Paul wanted. Through the cross, God had already separated Paul (and every other believer in Christ) from the body of this flesh. Now we can say with Paul, "If I therefore sin, it is no longer I that do it but sin that dwells in me" (see Rom. 7:17,20). To the unspiritual mind this sounds like a way to circumvent God's requirements. The truth is, our failure to see and believe is why we do not walk in the liberty Christ Jesus obtained for us through His death on the cross.

Reconciliation

In Romans 5:5 we find that "the love of God has been poured out within our hearts through the Holy Spirit who was given to us" (NAS). God's love in our hearts keeps us going. God has formed an intimate relationship within you from which you cannot escape. It is pressing you and motivating you. It is sending believers to the cross and from the cross to around the world with the "good news" about the God who loves sinful people. The love of God allows believers to get angry with God and live to go back to Him and apologize. It allows believers to get out of relationship with one another and then see that relationship restored. There is a motivating force within us that moves us to love one another. It is not saying to you, "You must love that brother or sister." It is working within you so you can learn to love them. Even if they do not love you in return, you still love them because it is "the love of Christ [that] constraineth you" (2 Cor. 5:14). That is what allows us to be reconciled to someone who refuses to be reconciled to us. Jesus, through the cross, reconciled Himself to His people even though they do not, in so many cases, want to be reconciled with Him.

Our Only Entry

If you were called to appear before the presence of the Lord right now, what would your attitude be? What is your first reaction when faced with the possibility of standing before God? "Is all clear between us? What have I been doing today? Have I missed anything in my confession?" Is that your first reaction? Suppose you determine that is not as it should be. Perhaps you think, "I cannot go before Him like this." If you cannot "go before Him like this," then there would never be a time when you could go before Him. If it is your own merit that you are trusting, then all is lost. If you cannot appear before Him when all is wrong, then you cannot appear before Him when all is right. "Not by works of righteousness which we have done, but according to His mercy He saved us" (Tit. 3:5a). Our sole authority to appear justified before Him is by the cross and by the blood Jesus shed upon that cross.

We are not in a less privileged position when everything is all wrong than when everything is all right. We only feel free to approach Him when we feel we have behaved rightly. In fact, when we think we have behaved rightly, God might see our behavior as all wrong. So we may be coming in arrogance without realizing the true state of our heart. Nevertheless, we are received on the basis of the blood of the cross.

Love gave the cross and the One who died on it. "God so loved that He gave" and "He that spared not His own Son, but delivered Him up for us all, how shall He not with Him also freely give us all things" (Jn. 3:16; Rom. 8:32). How grand a work, how magnificent a promise!

Yielding To That Love

Yielding to the Spirit is not simply doing everything right. Our desire to yield comes out of a redeemed heart. We yield to the Spirit of Christ that is in us and love becomes the driving force that sends us in the right direction, whether it be toward God or toward the brethren. When and if things go wrong (and they will), as I am walking in the Spirit and yielding to Him, I know that God will make it turn out right. I can get up from my fall and keep on walking. If I am summoned into His presence, I can stand before Him by the authority of the blood with confidence. The believer who comes into His presence on that basis, regardless of what kind of failure he is, will come before Him unashamed. That believer does not have anything to hide.

It has been said that the truly humble man can never be humiliated. There is no further "down" for him. He has already found out who and what he is, and he will be manifest in "that day" anyway. The things that are spoken in secret will be shouted from the housetops (see Lk. 12:3). We can be sure that what we hide in the darkness, God will bring into the light. We might as well settle it in our minds now that God has received us on the basis of what He has done, in spite of what we are and do and not because of it. Furthermore, by walking in the righteousness of God instead of our own, by recognizing the problem is present in us, by accepting God's provision through the cross, then we may freely believe if we sin, "it is no more I that do it, but sin that dwelleth in me" (Rom. 7:17). We can now walk in the freedom, liberty, joy, and peace of the Holy Spirit.

We know that when we come before Him, there will be nothing found that has not already been exposed. Nothing will be a "shock" to anyone, especially to God. "For we through the Spirit, by faith, are waiting for the hope of righteousness" (Gal. 5:5 NAS). It is not by the works of the law, but through the Spirit. That is the intent of Romans 8:3-4:

> *For what the Law could not do, weak as it was through the flesh, God did: sending His own Son in the likeness of sinful flesh and as an offering for sin, He condemned sin in the flesh, in order that the requirement of the Law might be fulfilled in us, who do not walk according to the flesh, but according to the Spirit* (Romans 8:3-4 NAS).

Love Hopes and Endures

I love my wife. I know that she loves me. How can I tell that she loves me? She does all those things that I like her to do without my having to tell her. I could hire a maid and get the same things done and, probably, subtracting one wife and four children, it would have been much cheaper. But our relationship is not one of a maid and employer. I could pay her for doing all those things and she would do her duty and that would be the end of it. As it is, she does all those things and more because we have a relationship in love. Faith works by love. She believes by faith. She married me by faith. She had faith in the fact that the marriage would be good and that I would be and do not only the expected or the necessary for her, but "much more," to use Paul's term. This is not a contract based on distrust, but a covenant based on trust. We "believed" each other.

Sadly, today people get married by contract. "You do this and I'll do that, and if we do not measure up, we will divorce." That makes it simple. It does not have to work by love because a contract is enforced by a law. God did not bring us into a legal relationship. He has brought us into a relationship based on love. Everything we do toward one another is based on love. My wife took marriage by faith and if love were not there, how sad the walk. The rough spots usually cause trembling, but love is the security of any marriage. A relationship in marriage is not built upon deeds, but on attitudes. Our heavenly Bridegroom, the Lord Jesus, spends a great deal more time on our attitudes than He does on our actions.

Law a Hindrance to Love

In Galatians 5:7 Paul says, "You were running well; who hindered you...?" (NAS) He was saying, "You were running the race in your lane, but someone pushed you out." Paul is making reference to the Grecian games. Remember our analogy in Chapter 1? Like our own races, the Grecians staggered the runners in their lanes to adjust for the difference in distance created by the curve. By making the adjustment, all run the same distance. At the signal the runners would start and the runners are required to stay in their lane. If the runner cuts the corner, he runs a shorter distance than the fellow next to him. He has departed from his lane. Paul said, "Someone pushed you out of your lane; someone has disqualified you." The Judaizers had come to put them back under the law. This would disqualify the believers, for the law made nothing perfect. The law could not bring them to the finish line.

Law cannot produce faith. In Galatians 3:5 Paul says, "He therefore that ministereth to you the Spirit, and worketh miracles among you, doeth he it by the works of the law, or by the hearing of faith?" This is a rhetorical question. The law quite evidently did not bring the Spirit of Christ to us. On the other hand Paul tells us that faith works by love (see Gal. 5:6). Only love, given birth by the Word of God, can cause faith to work in us and bring us to maturity.

Under Authority

The son is free; he is even free to fail. However, he is not free to be irresponsible. The Epistle to the

Hebrews, while revealing that the Hebrew Christians were released from the law, is also careful to point out the responsibility that all believers have to duly constituted authority. Hebrews 13:17 reads, "Obey them that have the rule over you, and submit yourselves: for they watch for your souls, as they that must give account, that they may do it with joy, and not with grief: for that is unprofitable for you."

The Scripture cites three levels of authority for the Christian, which are constituted by God. First is Christ; second is the eldership of His Church; and third is government.

The first is obvious and should need no further comment. Paul says in First Corinthians 9:21, "Being not without law to God, but under the law to Christ." The law of Christ is love. Love will chasten and correct. One of the four things profitable from Scripture is to give "instruction in righteousness" (2 Tim. 3:16). More literally, this could read "chasten in righteousness."

The second is the leadership that is ordained of the Lord. In the passage quoted from Hebrews 13:17, it is evident that someone should be responsible for my soul. These leaders are allowed into my life to a degree, so they can hold me accountable for my actions. To fail to acknowledge this authority could be "unprofitable." One of the gift ministries given by our Father to the local church is to the one who "rules." The idea in the Greek is to stand before as a leader or one who maintains. This one watches for my soul.

The third is civil government. With all of the ills present in the political systems of the Roman world, the writers of the New Testament never authorized, nor even encouraged, a rebellion against them. Every civil government will have its lesser and greater failures and injustices. Our response to them, however, is to walk without offense. Peter says that if we suffer as a Christian, we should be happy for it, but we should never suffer as an evil doer (see 1 Pet. 3:14,17). Paul tells us that the "powers that be are ordained of God. Whosoever therefore resisteth the power, resisteth the ordinance of God: and they that resist shall receive to themselves damnation" (Rom. 13:1-2).

There is no true liberty without authority. The character of the cross of Christ is submission to authority. The example which Christ left to us is to "let this mind be in you, which was also in Christ Jesus"; He "made Himself of no reputation" and "became obedient unto death." (See Philippians 2:5-8.) Christ at the cross is our example.

The Cross an Offense

Galatians 5:11 reads, "And I, brethren, if I yet preach circumcision, why do I yet suffer persecution? then is the offense of the cross ceased." Paul said that if he would simply add law to his message, he would no longer be persecuted. It would have been nice not to be persecuted, but then the truth would suffer. The cross is an "offense" because man insists on making his own contribution toward maturity. He would even include a contribution toward his redemption. In fact, the word translated "offense" comes into English from the word *scandal*. To preach total salvation through the cross, plus nothing, is a scandalous thing and utterly hated by the world and the flesh.

Walking in the Light of the Cross

Have you noticed how difficult it is to talk to people who are "spiritual"? There is a pseudo-spirituality that wants to represent itself as an example of maturity and spiritual success. Actually, it is obnoxious. It sets up a wall or a barrier to fellowship. The cross, on the other hand, exposes me for what I really am. The cross tells all of us what God thought of us apart from His work of redemption. There is a light in the cross that shows we are all in need of Him because we have no righteousness of our own. As long as a brother knows what I truly am, he will have no trouble fellowshipping with me.

Years ago I received quite a rebuke because I was coming on to another pastor as super-spiritual. In an effort to graciously point this out to me, he spoke in the third person, but the message was to me. "Keith, come on down where we can fellowship!" I thought, "What have I done?" Obviously I had given him the impression that I felt higher and more advanced in Christ than him. In order for him to communicate with me, he would have to "take a higher seat." What a hypocritical attitude this manifested in me! The law produces that sort of attitude.

In his Epistle to the Colossians, Paul said that all this outward show and legalistic pursuit only makes the flesh look good (see Col. 2:23). It will not allow true fellowship ("two fellows in the same ship"). It is lonely to live without true fellowship. On the other hand, if I know what you are and you know what I am, then we do not have any communication problems because we do not have anything to hide. In his first epistle John expresses this, saying, "But if we walk in the light, as He is in the light, we have fellowship one with another, and the blood of Jesus Christ His Son cleanseth us from all sin" (1 Jn. 1:7). Fellowship comes out of total honesty.

The End of the Matter

Paul said that Jesus Christ "is the end of the law for righteousness to every one that believeth" (Rom. 10:4). We sing, "Christ is all I need." But the question arises, "Is He all I want?" To walk at liberty is to know Christ in us is our only hope of life here and the glory that is to follow.

It has not escaped me that these few words are inadequate to convey the grand truth that is incorporated in Paul's message. It is my prayer, however, that He who is the Spirit of Truth will give us all such an illumination to all that we are and have in Christ Jesus, that our vision will no longer be upon ourselves and our efforts (whether successful or not). I also pray that He will so consume our thoughts so as to give us "no more conscience of sins" (Heb. 10:2); and that we would so come to know the love of

Christ; and that we would know that His chief desire is our good, that we would want naught but His glory.

May the God of all grace grant us all joy and peace in believing, and may we, His people, come to "glory only in the cross of our Lord Jesus Christ, by whom the world is crucified unto me, and I unto the world."

We will never be any more righteous than the blood of Christ can make us.

Once for All

Philip P. Bliss (1838-1876)

Free from the law O happy condition!
Jesus hath bled, and there is remission;
Cursed by the law and bruised by the fall,
Grace hath redeemed us once for all.
Now are we free—there's no condemnation!
Jesus provides a perfect salvation;
"Come unto Me—" O hear His sweet call!
Come—and He saves us once for all.
Children of God—O glorious calling!
Surely His grace will keep us from falling;
Passing from death to life at His call,
Blessed salvation—once for all.
Once for all—O sinner, receive it!
Once for all—O brother, believe it!
Cling to the cross, the burden will fall—
Christ hath redeemed us once for all!

**REST IN THE DAY OF
TROUBLE**
by Kelley Varner.
This book studies in detail the
prophecy of Habakkuk. Pastor
Varner shows the progression
of Habakkuk's expressing his
problem to his realizing the
provision—and so finding rest
in his day of trouble. We too
are in a day of trouble and,
like Habakkuk, can we find
rest in ours?
TPB-294p. ISBN 1-56043-119-9
Retail $9.99

IT'S TIME TO ROCK THE BOAT

by Michael L. Brown.

Here is a book whose time has come. It is a radical, noncompromising, no-excuse call to genuine Christian activism: intercessory prayer and the action that one must take as a result of that prayer.

TPB-210p. ISBN 1-56043-106-7
Retail $8.99

To order toll free call:
Destiny Image
1-800-722-6774

BORN TO TRIUMPH
by C. Paul Willis.
Read the story of Paul the apostle as it has never been told. Meet the man who could say, "It is no longer I who live, but Christ who lives in me!" Go with him on his travels, listen to him preach...and be changed as you see the Lord through the eyes of the apostle and bondservant, Paul.
TPB-392p. ISBN 1-56043-651-4
Retail $9.99

RAUL: A TRUE STORY
by Raul Gonzalez.
Raul would have sold his mother for a "hit" of heroin until he met Jesus Christ through Teen Challenge. Raul returned to the streets to witness for Christ, ministered to drug addicts in the U.S. military in Vietnam, and helped hopeless girls trapped in drug addiction, prostitution, and crisis pregnancies. This book is impossible to put down!
TPB-240p. ISBN 1-56043-777-4
Retail $6.99
(4¼" X 7")

To order toll free call:
Destiny Image
1-800-722-6774

MOMMY, WHY CAN'T I WATCH THAT TV SHOW?

by Dian Layton.

When Benjamin and Johnathan's mother turned off the television program they were watching, they wanted to know why. Their mom tells *them* a story that explains how important it is to guard what goes in their eyes and ears. Looking at good things brings wisdom, peace, and happiness; looking at wrong things lets ugly things inside.

TPB-24p. ISBN 1-56043-148-2 Retail $2.99
(8" X 9¹⁄₄")

MOMMY, WHY DID JESUS HAVE TO DIE?

by Dian Layton.

This is the book for every parent who wants to explain the salvation message to his or her child! In *Mommy, Why Did Jesus Have to Die?* Benjamin and Johnathan's mommy explains how Jesus came to earth to take our punishment and pay the price for our sins. In the end, Johnathan too becomes born again!

TPB-24p. ISBN 1-56043-146-6 Retail $2.99
(8" X 9¹⁄₄")

MOMMY, IS GOD AS STRONG AS DADDY?

by Barbara Knoll.

Daddies are always big and strong in little children's eyes, so that is how they think of their Father God. In *Mommy, Is God as Strong as Daddy?* little Robby learns that although Daddy is strong, God is even stronger.

TPB-24p. ISBN 1-56043-150-4 Retail $2.99
(8" X 9¹⁄₄")

MOMMY, WHY DON'T WE CELEBRATE HALLOWEEN?

by Linda Hacon Winwood.

Sometimes children ask the toughest questions! As a parent, you want to give them the best answers. This amazing children's book will help dedicated parents answer tough questions simply, biblically, and lovingly. Christ-centered and sensitively written, this book will help satisfy the curiosity of even the most inquisitive children.

TPB-24p. ISBN 1-56043-823-1 Retail $2.99
(8" X 9¹⁄₄")

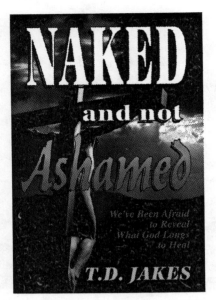